THE COMPETITIVE

GUNDOG

FIELD TRIALS AND WORKING TESTS

THE COMPETITIVE

GUNDOG

FIELD TRIALS AND WORKING TESTS

N. C. Dear

THE CROWOOD PRESS

First published in 2011 by
The Crowood Press Ltd
Ramsbury, Marlborough
Wiltshire SN8 2HR

www.crowood.com

© Nigel C. Dear 2011

British Library Cataloguing-in-Publication Data
A catalogue record for this book is available from the British Library.

ISBN 978 1 84797 282 8

Acknowledgments
I would like to thank Anne Greeves for proof reading the draft manuscript and for her many constructive criticisms. Thanks are also due to my daughter, Becky Dockeray, who despite the pressures of her own work managed to find the time to draw the diagrams. Together with the publisher, I would also like to thank Hilary Gould at the Kennel Club for permission to reproduce the 'J' regulations, Karolina Hedström at the Kennel Club Picture Library for her help in research and permission to reproduce images from the extensive archives, and also Nick Ridley and Penny Simpson for permission to reproduce their images.

Disclaimer
The author and publisher do not accept any responsibility in any manner whatsoever for any error or omission, or any loss, damage, injury, adverse outcome, or liability of any kind incurred as a result of the use of any of the information contained in this book, or reliance upon it.

Phoenix Typesetting, Auldgirth, Dumfriesshire
Printed and bound in Malaysia by Times Offset (M) Sdn Bhd

Contents

Introduction

The initial impulse to write this book was the realization that there was little, if anything, that covered working tests and field trials for gundogs in detail: what they are, what are they for, how they are run, how you run in them. Many gundog owners are very interested in the working possibilities of their dog but often don't know how to get involved, and whilst most are familiar with dogs working on a shoot, very few are aware of working tests or field trials.

But not all owners wish to work on shoots, or ever have the opportunity, and most are surprised to find that there are competitive and non-competitive events for them to train for, and take part in, outside the shooting environment. Unfortunately it is usually only those involved themselves in the working dog environment that get to know about these events – the average dog owner has little hope of finding out about them, and, it could be argued, anyway wouldn't be interested: it's a kind of Catch 22 situation.

The most common contact point for the new gundog owner is the training class, local gundog club or national training organization. Newcomers are key to the continued success of any sport, and it is incumbent upon us who are involved in our sport to actively encourage those who come along to train their dog – and not only to train, but also to educate and to foster active involvement in all the different field activities that are available. Explaining working tests and field trialling to them opens up new horizons to which an owner can aspire, providing a goal towards which their training can be directed. It is the newcomer, or uninitiated, to whom this book is directed.

Retriever, spaniel and the hunt, point, retrieve working tests and field trials are structured to reflect the working styles of the breeds and are therefore very different from one another. For this reason the book is structured in separate sections so those interested in learning about competing with a retriever, for example, have the subject covered in that section. This approach does lead to duplication of some aspects of a dog's work in the sections – the eye-wipe, for example – but effort has been made to minimize such duplication. Some parts of the text are relevant to other sections, particularly retrieving, but are not reproduced in them, again to avoid unnecessary duplication. The reader will therefore find much in the HPR section that is relevant to the retriever owner, and vice versa. The solution is to read the whole book! While researching the book the author attended a great many field trials and working tests, and found the whole experience to be highly interesting, very rewarding and definitely enlightening. To see the dogs enjoying their days out in very different ways was a delight, and I would encourage the reader to do the same.

Not all working gundog events are competitive: for example there are the spring pointing tests for HPR dogs designed to assess and improve quartering, and the Kennel Club's Working Gundog Certificate, which sets out to assess the working ability of a dog, recognizing those who can demonstrate that they are capable of carrying out the tasks required of them on the shooting field, either on a real shoot or a simulated environment using training dummies for retrieving and where no game is shot. Both these types of event are included here as they are still gundog events, participation in which will enhance both the handler's and the dog's experience of working, and providing more opportunity for both to be where they should be: out in the field together.

Chapter 1

Field Trials and Working Tests

WHAT ARE FIELD TRIALS?

A field trial is a competitive event, run in the manner of a shooting day, in which the dog's work on game is judged, and for which awards may be given for the best performance. If you aspire to your dog becoming a field trial champion able to use the prized FTCh prefix, this is where you need to be. Field trials are held for all the subgroups of gundog: retrievers, spaniels, pointers and setters and the hunt, point, retrieve (HPR) breeds, each subgroup having its own set of regulations governing conduct and organization.

Field trials are run under Kennel Club regulations (J) by the gundog clubs and societies

German wirehaired pointer at a Novice field trial, the starting point for all.

Field trials are run as a rough shooting day.

licensed to hold field trials, and are organized into stakes: Novice, All-Aged and Open. (The regulations are reproduced in Appendix A for reference, but it is important to know that they are revised annually, the latest version being published at the beginning of each calendar year; they are available from the Kennel Club for a nominal charge.) You start off in Novice trials and progress to All-Aged and Open trials, which represent the highest level of competition.

The starting point is the Novice stake, open to those dogs that have not gained a first in a Novice stake or an award in an All-Aged or Open stake. The All-Aged stakes are open to all dogs (although preference may be given to those with field trial awards), and are often perceived as a stepping stone to Open trials; they are judged as an Open trial would be, and are used by Open qualified dogs which the owner would like to

run in a trial, keeping the dog in current practice without taking up a precious place in an Open stake, or by dogs who may have won a Novice stake but need more experience before running in an Open.

Open trials are open to all dogs of the required standard, with preference given to previous performance. Win an Open trial, and your dog is on its way to becoming a field trial champion: this constitutes a first step, but further wins are required. If a spaniel, pointer, setter or HPR achieves another first it will become a FTCh, and winning a first or a second in an Open trial qualifies the dog to take part in a Championship Stakes. As you would expect, to achieve a first in an Open trial requires the dog to perform beautifully on the day, executing its tasks perfectly over two runs or rounds – which, as we shall see, is a real achievement indeed.

Championships are run annually and are contested by the '*crème de la crème*' of those competing during that season, with only the top performing dogs achieving the right to take part.

Field trials are not for everyone: although intended to be run as close to a normal rough shooting day as possible, they are in reality highly structured events quite often very far removed from the ordinary rough shoot. They are also testing, demanding the very best performance from your dog if he is to win a coveted field trial award at any of the stakes. And by training your dog to perform at the standard required in a field trial you will have a dog to be proud of, and one which will stand out as an exceptionally useful addition to any shooting party or shoot.

Some hold the view that if your dog is trained to perform its tasks well and can execute them correctly in the shooting field, then it should be good enough to compete in a field trial. Those who take part in field trials travel all over the country, sometimes setting off very early indeed to drive three or four hours to the venue, even the day before with an overnight stay if there is a particularly long journey in prospect – all in the knowledge that the dog could be eliminated in seconds for some misdemeanour, and be out of the trial completely. This does happen, though thankfully not too frequently, and does therefore demand a very philosophical approach, to be able to shrug one's shoulders and look forward to the next trial. But all the hard work, disappointments and misfortunes are forgotten when you experience the euphoria of winning your first award, with the concomitant life qualification to enter the field trial classes at Crufts, and entry in the Kennel Club stud book. You never forget the ground, who the judges were and how your dog ran.

Working tests use dummies instead of game.

Field trial competitors are noted for their good humour and sportsmanship, and in the company of other like-minded individuals, many of them real characters, you will have a memorable day out. Furthermore you will be competing alongside those who have become field trial champions and professional gundog trainers as well as the enthusiastic amateur, all committed to their dogs, so you will have the opportunity to listen, watch and learn with the best in the sport.

WORKING TESTS

Working tests are generally held out of the shooting season, with training dummies or cold game used for the retrieving tests instead of shot game. They are competitive events with awards given to the best performing dogs and handlers, and were originally devised to assess the progress of younger dogs, in particular to see how they were coming along during the summer months. First appearing as small, rather chaotic informal gatherings organized by the local gundog club, they grew rapidly in popularity, with the days becoming more structured and the participants learning from each other as increasingly they competed in a variety of events other than just the one organized locally, thereby fostering a cross-seeding of ideas and tests which improved as time went on.

Now there are literally hundreds of working tests held during the summer season, the majority at the weekends. They are organized and run under Kennel Club rules, and are

Working tests cater for all ages: a young Vizsla enjoys a day out.

extremely popular: whether you are interested in retrievers, spaniels or HPR dogs, there will be one that you can go to almost every weekend somewhere in the country.

The Kennel Club describes working tests as 'being best understood as a means to an end rather than an end in itself'. The distinction is that the working test is an assessment of a dog's working ability on that day, providing an indication of how it might perform in the shooting field – but the goal is still performance and improved performance in the shooting field, where the ultimate assessment will be made. Some competitors, however, view the working

---

FIELD TRIAL TRAINING DAYS

Many clubs and societies hold training days, sometimes called shotover days, aimed at those who have an interest in field trialling but don't know what is involved, and for those with young dogs to give them a chance to run as they would in a real trial, with Guns and judge, but without the eliminations that occur in a real trial. They are usually held at the beginning of the shooting season so that you have the opportunity to enter a real trial should your dog (and you!) prove to be about ready.

The aim is to give each dog at least two runs in the day, as would be the case in a field trial, and for this reason the entry is usually limited to no more than fifteen dogs; on some training days you may be lucky to get more than two runs, but don't count on it. A Kennel Club field trial judge will be present, just as they would be in a trial, but as well as judging your run they are there to act as a trainer for the day. This is invaluable if you are a beginner or still relatively inexperienced in trials or handling – remember that every field trial judge started out as a novice once, so they know how you feel.

Young dogs especially enjoy their day out.

test as an end in itself: many of those who attend working tests do so for the day out, the social occasion that it provides as well the chance to compete with their dog, and have no intention of setting foot on the shooting field; they do not shoot themselves but are happy to work their dog, which a good many of them do very profi-ciently. Whatever the interest or motivation of the dog owner, the working test welcomes and embraces all.

The question is often asked: 'How do I know if I and my dog are ready?' Unfortunately many trainers are not able to answer this question because they do not compete themselves in

---

In a real trial, dogs can be eliminated for various transgres-sions (described in the KC 'J' regulations governing field trials and working tests – *see* Appendix), such as unsteadiness, running in or chasing, missing game, as well as others, including whining. Were your dog to commit one of these faults in a real trial you would be asked by the judge to 'pick up' and that would be the end of your time in the trial, but at the training day, the judge would merely advise you of the fault, and tell you that you would have been eliminated, but will then allow you to continue until the allotted time has elapsed.

At the end of a run, the judge will be happy to give their critique on both the performance of your dog and of you, the handler. They will go through the run with you, pointing out where you might have done better as a handler, if you missed ground, where it was missed, and why. The dog may have missed game because you handled it in such a way that it ended up on the wrong side of the wind with no hope of scenting the game. The judge has the experience to be able to see these things and to articulate them to you to learn from. Even expe-rienced handlers make mistakes, and often it is because they are so concentrated on watching the dog that they miss the bigger picture, which the judge, being better placed, has the advantage of being able to observe.

At a training day you are not eliminated for transgressions.

either working tests or field trials. The easiest way to make an assessment is to go to one so you can see at first hand what happens, can watch the dogs work, see what the tests involve, and, crucially, talk to the competitors, who will be delighted to help you understand the sport. So often the interested but apprehensive newcomer is convinced that field trialling is for the professionals, and that he can't possibly aspire to that level of ability with his own dog – but this perception is easily dispelled, and a great many amateur trainers are competent to handle their dogs at the highest level.

It has often been stated that a dog that can acquit itself well in the shooting field is a potential field trial dog, and this is absolutely true. So don't rely on perceived prejudice, but use this book as your guide, and make the effort to go to

trials and working tests to see for yourself. Above all, get involved: you won't regret it, and you may be pleasantly surprised to see just how far you and your dog can go.

A SHORT HISTORY OF FIELD TRIALS

The first field trials took place in the mid-nineteenth century and were only for pointing breeds. The progress of the trial was dictated by the speed with which the muzzleloaders could be recharged – which was not very quickly, the average time to reload being about three minutes, and longer if something went wrong, which was a fairly frequent occurrence! However, when the breech-loading shotgun

Pheasant shoot, Illustrated London News 1884.

The curly coat, popular in the nineteenth century, but a rare sight today. (Courtesy Kennel Club Picture Library)

appeared towards the end of the 1850s, in particular with the convenience of the shotgun cartridge, the way gamebirds were hunted changed rapidly, and the number of birds shot increased dramatically. The development of the hammerless, self-cocking mechanism by Anson & Deeley in 1875 quickly made the hammer gun obsolete, and this, together with the more powerful smokeless Shultze powders, cartridge improvements that allowed tighter, harder-hitting patterns, cartridge ejector mechanisms, and a whole host of rapid technological advances, all combined to make a faster turnaround for the game shot – and even faster if the Gun had a matched pair of guns and a loader.

These developments meant that more birds than ever before were on the ground waiting to be picked up, and this also meant that a dedi-cated retrieving dog was needed. Flat-coated retrievers were used to start with, as there were plenty of them about, but the setter breeding in them favoured a long, curving outrun, using the wind as an air-scenting dog, which had two distinct disadvantages: first, the fact that the dog didn't go in a straight line to the retrieve wasted a lot of time; and second – and crucially – this curving outrun flushed other game which was probably out of range and thereby lost to the bag.

With these developments the spaniel came into its own. Spaniels had by this time already been divided into two different breeds, namely the cocker and the springer, and had moved on from flushing for the hawk to working in front of the gun while walking up. The cocker was used in likely woodcock-holding areas, usually open woodland, while the springer still worked open fields as well. Walked-up shoots suited the

Retriever field trial circa 1960. (Courtesy Kennel Club Picture Library)

spaniel, as birds flushed by the close-working dog were shot within easy retrieving distance and so a dedicated retriever that worked at long range was not needed any more.

Then with the advent of the driven shoot in the form of the *battue*, originally introduced from France, everything changed. The beater appeared, complete with bowler hat and stick, and the spaniel completed its transition to the role for which it is known today: quartering with its hallmark speed and drive in front of the bowler hats, pushing the birds ever forwards, and flushing into the air any that were sitting tight. Spaniel trials were first held in 1899, with retrieving competitions incorporated as part of these events (spaniels were not always required to retrieve at that time).

At this point in shooting history the Guns were escorted to their peg, in a fashion which, depending on the shoot, could be really grand or

fairly basic, in the back of a bone-shaking Land Rover MK I. Once installed at their peg, all they had to do was to wait patiently for the game to arrive in range overhead – which it did, in very large numbers indeed. With game now falling all over the place, retrieving it all became a major task in its own right, and so an efficient, calm, responsive retrieving dog became once again a major requirement. The exuberant flatcoat, never the steadiest or easiest to handle, had to be held by a dog man, and the curly-coated retriever – a rare sight now but common enough then – was equally unsuitable.

In the light of the requirement created by the new, popular shooting method, the biddable labrador, introduced in the mid-1850s and viewed hitherto with some condescension, slowly but surely made its way to the fore. With its superior marking, straight outrun and general willingness to please, by 1870 it was well established; it first appeared in a field trial in 1904, and by the time of the Great War was already the predominant retrieving breed, its efficiency providing the most persuasive of arguments even to those inevitable die-hards who so resented the wind of change that was sweeping through the sporting fields.

Field trialling played an important role in the development of all the breeds, with the best performing providing the benchmark to which others aspired, and those at the forefront very aware of needing to continually improve their own performance in a sustained effort to stay ahead of the quickly improving underdogs. Thus the competitive nature of the field trial contributed, as it still does today, to the field performance of the shooting dog.

And what of the hunt, point, retrieve (HPR) breeds? The first HPR dogs, then called pointer-

retrievers, were imported into the UK after World War II as a result of certain military personnel stationed in Germany learning of the very different type of hunting dog in use in that country, and of its impressive capabilities: these military people anticipated how useful it would be back home as a rough shooting dog.

Gradually the breeds started to become established in this country – and were the only example of pure breeds being imported for a specific purpose, rather than crossbred to add characteristics to a native breed. First to arrive were the German shorthaired pointer (GSP), the Weimaraner in 1952 and the Hungarian Vizsla in 1953, and the first field trial was held on 1 October 1955 by the German Shorthaired Pointer Club. For the next two decades or so the pointer-retriever continued to compete in utility trials against retrievers and spaniels (but

The GSP was the first HPR to be imported.

only in the retrieving tasks), and also in pointer and setter stakes in the autumn and spring.

Eventually the utility trials were abolished, and the newly renamed HPR gundogs were assigned their own separately regulated field trials by the Kennel Club. Competition has played as much a part in the improvement of the HPR breeds during the latter part of the twentieth century as it did with the retrievers and spaniels in the previous century, with equally dramatic effect. At the same time a greater understanding of the way an HPR dog works, along with the development of more specialist training – rather than treating the HPR as just another retriever – has led to vastly improved field performance and increasing approval from the hitherto largely sceptical shooting mainstream.

FIELD TRIALS TODAY

Trialling today still fulfils the function of improving breed performance, and indeed the most successful trial dogs are sought as breeding stock for subsequent generations. While it is a largely amateur sport, for the professional trainer and breeder achievement in the field adds a great deal of value to a dog, not only to its own resale value, but also to the price that can be asked for its progeny. This is by no means insignificant, since the demand for British-bred gundogs, both domestic and international, is very high indeed. One has only to look at the running card at international events to see the tremendous contribution made by UK-bred dogs.

In the main, however, it is the competition itself that attracts the committed amateur trialler, the taking part, the euphoria of winning, or the disappointment at being eliminated being all part of the experience. As with all competitions, the driving motivation is to prove yourself against your peers, taking the disappointments with good grace, but entering the next trial to go through it all again in pursuit of the ultimate goal: a field trial win.

At the time of writing, over 650 field trials were licensed in the shooting season, and the majority of them were oversubscribed, giving a clear indication of their popularity. There are ninety-eight retriever societies licensed to hold field trials which held 293 trials, eighty spaniel societies which held 238 trials, twenty-six pointer and setter societies holding forty-two trials, and twenty-six HPR societies holding seventy-two trials, the balance being made up with championship stakes.

Trials are commonly oversubscribed across all the subgroups (retriever, spaniel, pointer and setter, HPR), with the retriever group most of all, and Open stakes in particular being difficult to get a run in. One complaint often heard is that the same dogs and handlers appear to get runs in trials, the inference being that undue preference is given to these. What is often not appreciated, however, is that in Open and All-Aged stakes, the rules allow for preference in the draw to be given to dogs that have had previous successes, so these will have the advantage in that they will get a run based on their performance; this ensures that the very best dogs come to the top and are represented at the highest levels.

A field trial should follow, as closely as possible, a 'normal' day's shooting, which generally it does, even with the formalities of the running order, the presence of judges, and following the regulations under which the trials are run – not to mention the crowd of competitors, guests, the observers, the red flag, the steward, game carriers and spotters, all trailing along at a discreet distance behind! Retriever trials are held in both driven and walked-up categories, spaniel trials are usually held in woodland where their quartering drive and flushing abilities are best to be seen, the pointers and setters out on the big, wide fields of Norfolk or on the grouse moors, while HPR trials take place in all of those settings, underlining their versatile nature.

WHERE TO FIND A FIELD TRIAL

All field trials are licensed by the Kennel Club and are listed in the *Kennel Club Gazette*, published monthly, as well as being listed on the Kennel Club website. However, the listings are limited to the name of the society holding the trial, the field trial secretary and the name of the venue. Unfortunately no contact details other than the postal address of the field trial secretary are published, with the result that it is often difficult to find out where the trial is actually being held – the name of the venue may be listed, but not where it is located, not even the county! An internet search for the society will usually disclose contact details (telephone number, sometimes email address) from the website, enabling you then to make contact and ask about a specific trial, or to request their schedule, which will list all the trials that that particular society is holding during the season. Not everyone has access to the *Kennel Club Gazette* (although it is available by subscription to anyone), but there are other sources, notably the shooting press, with many of the magazines and periodicals carrying listings.

Normally one expects that the internet will provide an instant and comprehensive answer to virtually any question through a search engine, but those searching for field trials and working tests for spaniels and retrievers may well find themselves frustrated: a very large number of clubs and societies are listed – they are also listed on the Kennel Club website, and this includes more local societies as well as the national breed clubs – but trawling through them all to find their working event calendars and schedules is a daunting task. Furthermore it is not helped by the fact that even some of the larger national societies do not maintain their websites, with the result that much of the working information is out of date. Many of the smaller societies do not maintain websites at all, making it even more of a challenge to contact them easily or to find out what they have scheduled.

Those who trial frequently join many different clubs, for the simple reason that members usually enjoy a reduced entry fee for working events, and, very importantly, a member will be given preference over non-members in a trial entry. Retriever trials in particular are always oversubscribed, in that there are more entries than places available, and unless you are a member there will be no hope of getting a run – membership of at least twenty societies is probably the minimum necessary to be given the occasional run.

A further benefit of membership is that the schedules for field trials and working tests are posted or, more frequently nowadays, emailed to members. While this makes life a little easier for the club member, for the newcomer or the casually interested, it is still quite a task to find out what's on, and where. You will need to do some research, first with your local club – and do bear in mind that there will probably be several clubs in each county which may be contacted.

THE FIELD TRIAL GROUND

In order to run a trial the ground must be suitable for the purpose. In many cases, trials have been held on the same grounds literally for years, private shoots offering the ground to one society only, while commercial shoots are happy to hire out the ground to any society willing to pay for the birds shot. Most shoot grounds will lend themselves to run a trial, but it is important to ensure that a ground is suitable for the subgroup in question – one that is suitable for a retriever trial may not be so good for a spaniel or HPR trial. For this reason, if a new ground is offered to a society, the field trial secretary, along with an 'A' panel judge for the subgroup, will pay the ground a visit and inspect the proposed area together with the gamekeeper or host in order to determine its suitability.

It is highly desirable that the ground is

HPR trials always have a water retrieve.

contiguous – that is, that the field trial party can cover the whole area for the trial on foot, without having to use vehicles because some of the ground is some way away. While this might work for the Saturday shoot, in a trial it does interrupt the flow of proceedings, and more pertinently, it takes up valuable daylight time, always at a premium later on in the season.

The availability of game in the required numbers is also an important consideration, and must be addressed frankly with the gamekeeper beforehand. Retriever and spaniel trials will require a greater number of birds, and while the HPR trial will normally not require large numbers, the birds must be there for the questing dog to find, and ideally at a distribution density suited to the stake being run: thus in an Open HPR stake it is preferable for the dogs to have to work harder to find game, while in a

Novice stake too many birds can confuse a young dog, to the extent that it fails to point them correctly. The time of year can help in this decision, in that fewer birds are available later in the season, when an Open stake may be more appropriate.

The siting of stock fencing may also be crucial in that it may preclude retrieves, and be so positioned that it may not be possible to flush a pointed bird.

HPR trials require a water retrieve to be performed before a dog can receive an award, and those inspecting the ground should satisfy themselves that there is a body of water available on the ground, or not too far from it, and that it is fit for purpose – for example, that it is deep enough so the dog has to swim. Rivers and streams may be used but should be inspected to ensure a dog's safety.

Another consideration for the ground is the distance the dogs might be from roads when out working – a dog that decides to take off after a hare may well find itself a long way from where it should be, and if this involves crossing a busy main road, the consequences could be tragic.

On a practical level, access and parking are an issue for the many vehicles that will arrive, bearing in mind that not all of them will be four-wheel-drive.

A survey of the proposed ground is therefore absolutely vital to ensure that it is suitable, and it is equally important that it is carried out by those with substantial experience of running or judging the type of trial being considered.

The Cost of the Ground

In the past, landowners were happy for a society to run a trial on their shooting grounds without any charge or cost to that society. This is still very often the case today, particularly when the shooting ground is not being run as a commercial enterprise. In the latter case, however, a charge will be made to the society based on the number of birds that might be expected to be shot on the day. The society can recover this amount by charging the Guns, which usually works out to be a good deal for them; there is therefore generally little difficulty in finding Guns willing to do this, and the cost of the trial is easily offset.

This works well for retriever and spaniel trials where the number of birds shot can give the Guns a good day's shooting, but not always in HPR trials. Here the number shot is comparatively low – twenty-five birds shot during the whole trial would be considered a lot – and between two to four Guns this would be an expensive day out for relatively little sport. This

Paying Guns can help offset the cost of the trial.

is because of the way an HPR trial works, in that the dog must first find and point game, then flush it into the air, when it may be shot for the dog to retrieve. In most cases a single bird will be flushed, although there could be more, especially at the end of a game strip where birds will congregate, having run on in front of the questing dog. In addition, the judges will usually tell the Guns only to shoot birds that have been pointed by the dog in the first round, which again limits their chances of adding to the bag.

Thus Guns invited to shoot at an HPR trial must be aware of the need to shoot for the benefit of the dog (and the trial), and not for their own personal bag. Those who shoot regularly at these trials do so in the full knowledge of these limitations, and because they enjoy the discipline of shooting over the dog and having the unique opportunity of seeing these dogs work. Those who are shooting for the first time at such a trial should be aware of these limitations, and should be fully briefed by the judges as to when they should take a shot, and when not.

The society running the trial will always give due recognition to the support of the landowner: his name will appear on the running card, and he will be acknowledged verbally, both in the introductory remarks at the start of the trial, and again at the very end after the awards have been presented. It is also normal practice to present a small gift to the landowner or their nominated representative, irrespective of whether a separate payment has been made. After all, it is only with the patronage of the landowner that trials can take place at all, and we must never lose sight of their invaluable and continuing contribution to our sport.

ENTERING A FIELD TRIAL

To enter a field trial you must obtain an entry form from the field trial secretary of the promoting society, or download it from the website. The entry form is of a standard format approved by the Kennel Club (*see* Appendix) and must be filled in completely, signed and sent along with the appropriate fee back to the field trial secretary, preferably well before the date for the close of entries, which will be found on the schedule. It is important to enter the stud book number if you have one for your dog, and any qualifications it has – that is, any field trial awards, the place gained (first, second, third, fourth or CoM), along with the society and date of the trial where the award was gained.

This is important because field trial awards affect how your entry is treated in the draw if the trial is oversubscribed. If the entrant is from outside the UK, then an 'authority to compete' (ATC) number must be obtained from the Kennel Club and entered in the form. In the case of oversubscription, where the number of entries received exceeds the number of places available, there is a ballot procedure – in the simplest case, if there are fifteen entries and twelve places available, all fifteen go into a hat and the first twelve entries drawn out will be given a run in the trial. The unlucky ones make up the list of reserves.

However, certain criteria may be applied to give an entry preference in the draw over others; for example, preference might be given to members of the society, so their entries would go into the hat first. If there happen to be exactly twelve members entered for a twelve-dog trial, then all those entries will be allocated runs, and will go into the hat and be drawn in order to determine the running order of the dogs on the day. Any non-members entered will go into the list of reserves.

Other criteria may apply and will be stated in the standing instructions published by the society; these are usually the same across all societies, but there may well be variations (particularly relating to All-Aged stakes) so you must refer to those relating to the trial you wish to enter. The standing instructions, schedule and entry form are all available from the field trial secretary and from the website.

In the case of an Open stake, the preferences for the draw are laid down by the Kennel Club, and are as follows:

Retrievers: First, second, third or fourth place in a twenty-four dog Open stake, or first, second or third in a twelve-dog Open stake. First place in an All-Aged or Novice stake.

Spaniels: First, second or third in an Open stake, or first in an All-Aged or Novice stake.

HPRs: First, second or third in an Open stake; first or second in an All-Aged stake; first in a Novice stake.

What this means is that a dog entered which has one of the awards listed will take preference in the draw over other entries. In addition a society may give preference to its members, such preference being applied in the order of:

* members' dogs that have gained any of the awards listed above
* non-members' dogs with awards listed above
* members' dogs which have gained other awards
* non-members' dogs with other awards
* any other dogs

In the case of two dogs being entered with similar qualifications, the preferred dog must be indicated on the entry form (either by circling the dog's entry, or by a star next to the entry, otherwise the dog entered in the box marked 1 will be taken to be the preferred dog). In the case that there is an oversubscription for a twelve-dog stake, all the entries with those qualifications will be entered into a ballot but only the preferred dog(s) go into this first ballot. If this sounds confusing, the following example is given to illustrate the process of the draw to arrive at the dogs which will be offered a 'run':

Entries received for a twelve-dog Open stake:

Mr Smith, a member with one dog with a first in Novice

Mr Winters, a non-member with one dog with a first in All-Aged

Mrs Shaw, a member with one dog with a CoM in a Novice stake

Miss Blyth, a member with two dogs, one with a fourth in an Open stake and indicated as the preferred dog, the second dog with a first in a Novice stake

Mr Davis, a non-member with one dog with no awards

Mrs Davies, a member with one dog with no awards

Mr Peters, a member with one dog with a 1st in Novice

Mr Fry, a member with two dogs, none having awards

Mr Green, a member with one dog with a first in Novice.

Miss Hove, a member with one dog with a first in Novice

Mrs White, a member with one dog with a third in an Open stake

Mr Drew, a member with one dog with no awards

Mrs Curry, a member with one dog with a first in an All-Aged

There are fifteen entries for a twelve-dog stake, so a ballot must take place. Applying the rules above, first identify those dogs which are members with a qualifying award; these are Mr Smith, Miss Blyth's first dog, Mr Peters, Mr Green, Miss Hove, Mrs White, Mrs Curry. All these seven dogs will get a run and go into the hat. There are still five places available, so now apply the rules again to the remaining dogs:

Mr Winters, a non-member with one dog with a first in an All-Aged

Mrs Shaw, a member with one dog with a CoM in a Novice Stake

Miss Blyth, the second dog with a first in a Novice stake

Mr Davis, a non-member with one dog with no awards

Mrs Davies, a member with one dog with no awards

Mr Fry's dog one, a member with no awards

Mr Fry's dog two, a member with no awards

Mr Drew, a member with one dog with no awards

Of these, Miss Blyth's second dog is selected, as the rules state that a second similarly qualified dog(s) go into a separate ballot before dogs from other categories. As Miss Blyth's second dog is the only one to fall into this category, it will be selected to get a run. So now those getting a run are Mr Smith, Miss Blyth's first dog, Mr Peters, Mr Green, Miss Hove, Mrs White, Mrs Curry, and Miss Blyth's second dog.

This gives eight dogs with runs, leaving a further four to be selected from the following:

Mr Winters (non-member with a listed award)

Mrs Shaw (member with another award)

Mrs Davies (member, with no award)

Mr Fry's dog one (member, no award)

Mr Fry's dog two (member, no award)

Mr Drew (member, no award)

Mr Davis (non-member, no award)

Applying the rules again, Mrs Shaw and Mr Winters both gain preference over the others so can be selected for a run; this list is now Mr Smith, Miss Blyth's first dog, Mr Peters, Mr Green, Miss Hove, Mrs White, Mrs Curry, Miss Blyth's second dog, Mrs Shaw, Mr Winters.

This is ten dogs, leaving two more to be selected from the remainder:

Mrs Davies (member, no award)

Mr Fry's dog one (member, no award)

Mr Fry's dog two (member, no award)

Mr Drew (member, no award)

Mr Davis (non-member, no award)

Mr Fry's first dog goes into a separate ballot with Mrs Davies, Mr Drew and Mr Davis. This ballot is drawn, and Mrs Davies and Mr Fry's first dog come out of the hat and are added to the previously selected ten dogs to make up the twelve dogs that will definitely get a run in the trial. These twelve are all put into the hat and are then drawn to yield the number that they will appear on the running order. The result of the draw and the running order on the day is:

Miss Hove

Mrs Curry

Miss Blyth's second

Mr Smith

Mrs Shaw

Mr Fry's first

Mr Green

Mrs Davies

Miss Blyth's first

10. Mr Peters

11. Mr Winters

12. Mrs White

The remaining dogs (Mr Fry's second, Mr Drew, Mr Davis) will make up the reserve list, but go into another ballot to determine their reserve number. As members, Mr Fry and Mr Drew get preference so they are drawn first: Mr Drew comes out first and is therefore assigned first reserve, Mr Fry becomes second reserve and Mr Davis third reserve. Thus the full list that makes up the card for the day is as follows:

1. Miss Hove
2. Mrs Curry
3. Miss Blyth's second
4. Mr Smith
5. Mrs Shaw
6. Mr Fry's first
7. Mr Green

8. Mrs Davies
9. Miss Blyth's first
10. Mr Peters
11. Mr Winters
12. Mrs White

Reserves
13. Mr Drew
14. Mr Fry
15. Mr Davis

Note that in practice the Kennel Club-registered name of the dog appears on the draw along with the name of the handler; surnames were used here only to illustrate the process of making the draw. It is quite a complex process, but luckily for the field trial secretary who has to organize it, the rules for Novice and All-Aged stakes are much simpler and correspondingly easier to do. The draw usually takes place about a week or ten days before the date of the trial itself in order to give those with runs time to make arrangements to take time off work, book hotel accommodation, and so on. Detailed directions to the meeting place are given at the same time.

This final list of runners and reserves constitutes the 'draw' and will be the running order on the day of the trial. It will be sent to all entrants either by post or by email; if you don't receive any notification you can always call or email the field trial secretary to find out whether or not you have a run. For pointers and setters the procedure is similar, but a further draw is done at the start of the trial itself; this is detailed in the pointer and setter trials section.

Nomination Method

Retriever trials are normally well oversubscribed, with sixty-plus entries for a twelve-dog stake not uncommon (and in the order of 150-plus entries for a twenty-four dog, two-day Open qualifying stake). In order to reduce paperwork, some societies adopt the nomination method of entering a trial, and if this is the case, it will appear on the trial schedule (*see* the sample schedule in the Appendix, page 159). At the bottom of the schedule there is a slip to complete, cut out and send to the field trial secretary, along with a small, non-returnable fee: this is your 'nomination' and serves to get your dog(s) entered into the draw. The draw is completed in the usual way, and the lucky twelve who have been pulled out of the hat are notified by email or post and are now asked to complete the field trial entry form and send it, along with the entry fee, back to the field trial secretary. Receipt of the entry form and fee will confirm the run is being taken up.

If the entry form is not received by the field trial secretary it will be assumed that the run is not being taken up and one of the reserve dogs will be contacted; usually the field trial secretary will attempt to contact the missing entrant by telephone or email in case something has gone wrong with the post, but they are under no obligation to do this, and it is really up to the entrant to ensure the entry gets to the field trial secretary in good time.

The principal advantage of this method is that it saves cheques and entry forms being made out and sent off unnecessarily; sixty-plus unused cheques being simply destroyed is just a waste, plus the postage cost, and when it is considered that many such entries will have to be made in search of that elusive run, the number of wasted cheques is multiplied many times, with a considerable end cost to the increasingly impecunious competitor. Some consider that this method over-complicates the issue and is merely a way of extracting more money from the competitor. Furthermore it may be that with the decline of the cheque (and many institutions are now refusing to take them) an alternative method of taking payment will be necessary – bank transfer, for example.

Contact Details

Make sure that you provide contact details on the form which are readable and actually work. It is quite a task to decipher some people's hand-writing – email addresses in particular can be very difficult to understand, and if the electronic address is in any way incorrect, anything sent that way will bounce back or disappear for ever into the cyber ether. Any telephone number you provide, whether mobile or landline, should actually help to reach you at any time. I write this with some feeling as a field trial secretary who has attempted to contact handlers at short notice on the reserve list (because someone has with-drawn) to offer them a run at the trial in question, only to find that they are not reach-able, their mobile is turned off, there is no voicemail service to leave a message, the home number is not answered, and so on.

It is in your best interest to be contactable, particularly as the day of the trial nears when most withdrawals seem to occur, even on the night before the trial. The field trial secretary will do his or her very best to get in touch with you, but when the date of the trial is very close there is no time to be wasted and the run will inevitably go to the one on the list that could be contacted in time. The evening before one trial I went through seven reserves before I found one that was available, and the person concerned was delighted: they had thought that because they were so far down the reserve list there would never be any prospect of getting a run. And to add to the delight, that particular dog and handler came away with a field trial award!

THE JUDGES

Field trials are officiated by two to four judges, depending on the trial being conducted. There must be at least one Kennel Club 'A' panel judge, the other(s) being either another 'A' panel, then 'B' panel, or so-called non-panel

---

THE SHOW GUNDOG WORKING CERTIFICATE

For the show champion (ShCh) dog to have the 'Sh' removed and be designated 'Champion', it must demonstrate some ability in the shooting field either by competing in and winning an award at a field trial, or being awarded a Show Gundog Working Certificate. The SGWC is available for all gundog subgroups and can be obtained by participating in a field trial or a dedicated Show Gundog Working Certificate day. To enter for a SGWC at a field trial, the field trial secretary should be contacted beforehand to ask whether such an entry would be accepted: some societies and judges do not accept SGWC entries, so it is necessary to check. If it is acceptable, then an entry into the trial must be made in the usual way on the standard field trial entry form; it is a good idea to write 'SGWC' on the form as a reminder to the field trial secretary. The entry will treated as separate from the other entries and is not subject to ballot in the case of the main body of the trial being oversubscribed. It is entirely up to the judges when the SGWC dog is brought into line, and they will choose a convenient point in the trial to do so; it could be at any time in the middle of the trial, and not neces-sarily at the end, after all the other dogs in the trial have run, which is often the assumption.

Unlike the other dogs in the trial which will be required to perform multiple retrieves or have at least two runs, the SGWC candidate only needs to be tested in line once. For retrievers, the ability to hunt for, locate and retrieve dead or wounded game from cover to hand must be demonstrated. Spaniels must hunt, face cover, flush game and retrieve to hand; pointers and setters must hunt and point game, and HPR dogs hunt, point and retrieve, all to the satisfaction of the judges. The retrieving breeds are also required to perform a retrieve from water, to demonstrate that they can enter water, swim and retrieve (usually a pigeon, but if game is not available a dummy may be used). Dogs are expected to be under reasonable control at all times, but are not expected to demonstrate the same level of steadiness required of the field trial competitor.

(NP) judge, depending on the stake being run. The function of the judge is to interpret the dog's run in terms of the field trial regulations, and to assess the performance of the dog on the day. The judges work as a team, in that each will make their own individual assessment of a dog's performance, but they may confer with each other when a critical decision has to be made. The assessment of the run is recorded in a book that each carries, as a letter grade. They will also make notes to keep a tally on what the dog has done and what it may have to do in any subsequent rounds – for example an HPR may need to have a point on a bird, a retriever might not have been shot over to test steadiness.

Judges, as you would expect, are highly experienced, not only at judging but also in field trials: as competitors, each judge will have years of experience in both. When starting out, the prospective judge has to be invited to judge by a club or society licensed to hold field trials. Societies usually have a set of minimum criteria that the prospective judge must fulfil before he can be considered as a judge for them; these will certainly include many years of field trial experience (the Kennel Club recommends at least five years), to have won a number of field trial awards, experience of work in the shooting field, and others which usually include judging at working tests. Prospective HPR learner

judges are encouraged to have judged a spring pointing test, where they will be introduced to assessing a dog's quartering performance from a judging perspective, working with an 'A' panel judge who will act as mentor for the day as well as acting as the senior judge at the event. The working test season continues right through the summer, providing prospective judges with further opportunities either to judge a class by themselves or to learn how it is done.

The new judge can expect to be given the first judging appointment by a club chosen by the judge to promote him or her throughout the learning phase. When the first appointment has been completed, the learner or non-panel (NP) judge will be allocated a judge's number by the Kennel Club, which must subsequently be published alongside his name on the field trial programme. Now on the ladder, the NP judge must now judge at least four trials under four

Judges assess all aspects of a dog's work.

different 'A' panel judges over a minimum of three years, after which time an application to join the 'B' panel can be made. The 'A' panel judge provides a written assessment of the 'B' panel or NP judge (whichever happens to be the co-judge for the day) to the Kennel Club, and these assessments are taken into consideration when deciding whether a judge may be admitted to a panel. To become an 'A' panel judge will require the 'B' panel judge to judge a further six trials under five different 'A' panel judges, with at least one Open stake. In all cases the applicant must be able to demonstrate that they have substantially increased their field trial experience as a competitor.

Every field trial judge is expected to be fully conversant with the latest 'J' regulations that govern field trials, as these do change from year to year. The Kennel Club introduced a system in 2007 whereby presenters approved by the KC deliver prepared presentations on the current regulations, followed by a written examination, in order to provide a common base of up-to-date knowledge. Anyone aspiring to be a field trial judge will have to pass this examination (as do current 'B' panel judges who have to pass before they can be considered for promotion to the 'A' panel); this initiative has been well received, with many competitors also attending these presentations and taking the exam.

ON THE DAY

Armed with your directions to the trial and ensuring you have the vital components of dog, whistle and lunch with you in the car, set off in good time, aiming to arrive at least fifteen minutes before the published start time; building in some delay time is always a good idea, because arriving late can have dire consequences, as we shall see. On arrival, report to the field trial secretary or the chief steward, who can be readily identified as the most harassed-looking individual, with a pile of papers and other paraphernalia on the back of their car. You will be issued with a numbered armband that corresponds to your place in the trial running order, and a field trial programme which lists the running order of the dogs, including the reserves, along with dog and owner details.

About ten minutes before the trial is to begin, the chief steward will check that all the dogs and handlers are present, and if they are not, will inform the judges who may need to make a decision nearer the time the trial is scheduled to start as to whether or not to exclude someone who hasn't made it by this time. If a handler is not present at the time the trial is deemed to have started, their run can be forfeited and the first reserve called upon to take the missing dog's place, assuming their number. If the handler concerned calls to say that they are experiencing some problem, and if they give a reasonable ETA, this may help their case, but usually the judges will take a dim view of lateness, given that all the other handlers, Guns and so on, not to mention the judges themselves, very obviously managed to get there on time.

If there are reserves present who can be called up, this is an easier decision to make for the judges, but if not, they may elect to allow the trial to continue as long as the missing competitor appears in time to take up his run when his number is called. Clearly, if they are number eleven dog, in a spaniel or HPR trial it can be some considerable time until they are called for; but in a retriever trial, all dogs may well be called into line together for a steadiness drive. If there is a shortage of dogs, there may be competitors who have a second dog in the car who may wish to enter, or indeed someone local to the trial may have turned up 'on spec' with a dog in the hope that just this situation will arise. In these cases, a dog may be entered on the day, though this has to be with the agreement not only of the judges but also of the competitors. A field trial entry form must then be completed and the entry fee paid before the handler can

Collect your armband and running order from the chief steward.

compete – the chief steward will have spare entry forms available for this eventuality.

Just before the trial is scheduled to start, the chief steward will call everyone together and perform the preliminaries: he will welcome everyone to the trial, introduce the host (if present), the steward of the beat, judges, Guns, picking-up dog and the person who carries, and is known as, the red flag. Any changes to the field trial programme are announced, as are withdrawals or no-shows, and any reserves or late entries, who, by virtue of being present, are now allocated the number(s) for those runs not being taken up. A safety briefing is given, reminding those present that they should remain at all times behind the red flag when not in line, and attention is drawn to the society's field trial risk assessment.

The chief steward will also advise arrangements for lunch, whether a suitable break is planned, or more usually that lunch will be 'on the hoof' and competitors should take something with them. Remember that as daylight hours become increasingly restricted as the season progresses the judges will want to make maximum use of the available light and not waste time with extended lunch breaks.

The judges will be called upon to make any opening remarks, and in a Novice stake they will normally ask if there is anyone present who has not trialled before, and to identify themselves when they come into line.

With these formalities complete, the trial can start and everyone will move off to the trial ground.

Steward of the Beat

The steward of the beat is responsible for providing the trial with the ground over which the dogs will run, using knowledge of the ground to ensure, as far as is possible, that sufficient birds are available to test the dogs. The steward of the beat is usually the gamekeeper or nominated representative, and occasionally the landowner. Many will host a number of trials throughout the season and are therefore well acquainted with the requirements of the trial.

The Red Flag

Those competitors who are waiting to run their dog, along with any spectators, constitute the 'gallery' which follows behind the line, generally a body of at least fifteen people. The person designated to be the 'red flag' carries a red flag on a stick, the purpose of which is to provide a clear indication of the position of the gallery for the benefit of the Guns in order for them to assess the direction of a safe shot. Ideally the gallery should keep together in a close group, but very often it becomes strung out over a distance as members get involved in private conversations, not noticing that the rest have moved on. This is unsafe, and often the worst offenders are those who should know better, and it is the red flag's task to remind them to keep together.

The red flag will also liaise with the chief steward and the steward of the beat as to the best position for the gallery and its movements in order to keep a safe position, but also so that the gallery can be kept as close to the action as possible so they can see the dogs running.

The red flag and steward of the beat confer.

The Picking-Up Dog

Kennel Club regulations dictate that there should be present throughout the duration of the trial a dog and handler whose sole purpose is to search and find wounded game that cannot be collected by those dogs running in the trial itself. One dog and handler is usual, although there may be more than one at some retriever stakes. The judges can call upon the picking-up dog at any time during the trial, most commonly to go and look for a bird which has been seen to have been hit but has flown a considerable distance, useless for the purposes of the trial, but which nevertheless must be collected. Another instance might be where a bird has been seen to be a strong runner, wounded but still very mobile – usually one of the dogs in the line will be sent promptly for such a case, but there are circumstances where it is of no value to the trial and the judges will quickly signal for the picking-up dog to go for it.

It is worth making it absolutely clear that the regulations call for a dedicated picking-up dog to be appointed, and that to rely on dogs discarded from the trial is not an acceptable practice – apart from the breach of the rules, it could be that the services of the picking-up dog are called upon early on in the trial before any dogs have been discarded. What would happen then? It is therefore an important task in its own right, and cannot be deputized in this way.

The amount of work the picking-up dog is required to do is completely variable: there may be many occasions when it is not called upon at all, and others when it is kept very busy indeed. It is usual for the handler to receive a gratuity for his time.

END OF THE TRIAL: AWARDS

Those dogs that make it successfully to the end of the trial (including completing their water test if required) may be eligible to receive a field

A picking-up dog must always be ready.

trial award. This could be a first, second, third or fourth place, or a certificate of merit (CoM). The judges are not under any obligation to award a particular place if they feel that the required standard has not been met, and are quite at liberty to withhold a place. So, for example, they may decide to award a first, a third and a fourth along with two CoMs, but to withhold the second place; at another trial a single fourth might be awarded, or no awards at all. The judges communicate their decision to the chief steward, who will then make arrangements for place certificates to be made out in the name of the dog, countersigned by the judges who will also sign a game certificate, which certifies to the Kennel Club that sufficient game was present during the trial.

Finally the steward will call everyone

Field trial winners, with judges.

together for the awards ceremony. He will ask the judges to make any comments or observations about their day and the performance of the dogs and handlers, and will thank the host for the use of the ground, the Guns for their expertise, and the red flag and picking-up dog for their time spent fulfilling these inglorious but necessary functions. The judges, in making their remarks, will thank the society for inviting them to judge, as well as the host, the keeper and the Guns. They may make general remarks about the standard of dog work, the prevailing conditions, and the possible impact on the trial, but they are not required to make an individual appraisal of the performance of any one dog or handler. It is usual for the winner to make a short speech, thanking the host, Guns, judge and fellow competitors.

Those with awards will rejoice in their success in the knowledge that they, in partnership with their dog, have successfully completed the most testing of any kind of trial; and those who were not lucky enough to make it this time will have learned a little more about trialling, themselves and their dog, which will help them be one of those in the awards at a future trial.

Chapter 2

Retriever Field Trials

THE RETRIEVER'S TASK

On the face of it, the task of the retriever is simply stated: to retrieve fallen game to the handler. Of course it is much more than that, as the dog is expected to sit quietly next to its owner at his peg on the driven shoot, only going off to retrieve a fallen bird when told to do so, and to sit there so that the owner does not have to worry about what the dog is up to, leaving his mind completely free to concentrate on the shooting. The dog must be completely trustworthy – a good peg dog.

The rough shooter, by contrast, will be walking along alone or in the company of a few others, and expects the dog to walk along beside

The retriever's job is to find and deliver fallen game to hand.

Runners must always be retrieved first.

him, stopping and sitting when he stops either to take a shot or because someone else in the party has done so. The 'no-slip' dog is so termed because it is reliably steady when off the lead (slip). In either case, whether the shoot is rough or driven, the dog is expected to wait for the command from its handler to make the retrieve.

You may wonder why this is important, but there are good reasons for steadiness to be very high on the list of things the dog must master. Consider the situation in which a rough shooter, walking along with the dog, spots a rabbit suddenly bolting away: he raises his gun and starts to take a bead on the rabbit, when the dog decides to give chase – and the shooter, afraid of hitting the dog instead of the rabbit, must abandon the shot, the chasing dog thereby robbing him of an addition to the bag.

On the driven shoot, fallen game is collected at the end of the drive, signalled either by the head beater yelling 'All out!', the shoot captain's whistle or hunting horn, or both. Then the business of collecting the birds starts in earnest, the Gun's own dog possibly dispatched to fetch those that are within easy distance, or which the Gun has seen fall further away but wishes his dog to retrieve. The Gun, as a paying customer, has a perfect right to use his dog to retrieve as many birds as he sees fit, but in practice most Guns get the easiest retrieves before packing up and hurrying off to the next drive.

The members of the picking-up team, lined up some way behind the Guns, now start their task. A good retriever will be capable of 'marking' the exact position of the point of fall of a particular bird, remembering it even when it marks another fall, and it should be able to retrieve multiple marks when asked to do so.

Even the best dog has its limits, however, and although the shooter may well have some idea of where some of the birds he has shot have fallen, his primary task is to shoot game; therefore the responsibility falls only in part on the dog at his side, but in the main on the picking-up team. Wounded game, 'runners' or 'pricked' birds must be located and despatched as soon as possible, and the picking-up team will be watching, eagle-eyed, and will send one of their dogs immediately to recover such game.

For the field trial dog, steadiness – the capacity to sit and wait for the command to retrieve – is of paramount importance. Ideally the dog will be completely steady whatever the situation, and certainly a dog competing in an All-Aged or Open trial will be expected to be so, though some latitude will be allowed for the Novice stake dog; but a dog whose tail end is in front of the handler's knee will be close to being eliminated, and even if the judges let it go, it will be noted by them and will count against the dog in the final reckoning. And a dog that 'runs in' – dives off uncommanded to retrieve – will be eliminated immediately.

In a driven trial, birds are driven over the Guns with the competing dogs behind, and large numbers of birds may be shot, with some falling quite close to the dogs. Being steady in such circumstances is quite a test, particularly for the young novice. In a walked-up trial birds may be shot at all possible angles, in front as well as behind, and it is by no means the case that a dog will be sent for a bird that has fallen directly in front of it. Indeed, it is highly likely that it will instead be sent for one in front of another dog in the line, having to ignore the one nearest to it in order to retrieve the one requested by the judges, thereby demonstrating its steadiness and good training.

Dogs are expected to sit quietly in line: any whining, yelping or 'squeaking' is unacceptable, and judges will have no hesitation in eliminating the dog from the trial. Young, very keen dogs are the worst offenders, especially when they want

to get at the retrieve but have to wait, frustrated, for their turn: watching others having the fun is often too much for them, and the quiet whine becomes more persistent, finally escaping as a yelp. If this happens at a trial, the dog will be out.

The field trial will therefore test the dog in this environment, its overall performance watched over and assessed by the judges.

JUDGING SYSTEMS

For Retrievers there are two different judging systems, one with three judges and the other with four, the latter being the system most used today.

The Three Judge System

In the three judge system the field is split equally between the judges, with dogs one and two going to the judge placed on the right of the line, three and four to the middle judge, and five and six to the left-hand judge. If there is one 'A' panel judge present they will take up position in the middle so as to be more available to the other judges if needs be, and also so they can keep an eye on what is going on along the whole line. The judges will decide among themselves their position in the line before the trial begins, informing the chief steward as a courtesy.

The chief steward will make up the line by calling up the competitors in numerical order and sending them up to stand with their judge, and positioned on the correct side with numbers ascending from the right of the line. If dog three is eliminated, the chief steward or dog steward will send the next dog (number seven) forward to fill the space in the line. If no dogs are eliminated and all have successfully made their allotted number of retrieves, the whole line will be replaced with dogs seven to twelve. In the first two rounds dogs must be seen by more than one of the judges, so the dog steward has to keep track of which dog has been seen by which judge. In subsequent rounds, dogs remaining in the trial must be sent up to the line in numerical order to any one of the judges that has a vacancy. It is not necessary for a dog to be seen by all three judges, although this may happen, but it must have run under at least two at some time during the trial.

However, this system has largely been replaced by the four judge system, and is now seldom employed. The main reason is that if only one 'A' panel judge is present it may be difficult or impossible for him to keep an eye on the other judges, particularly if they are out of sight, and an inexperienced non-panel judge judging alone and without the guidance of a peer could make a wrong or bad decision. Also, each judge has to keep an eye on both dogs currently in line, and it may not be an easy matter to watch a dog working out in front of the line assessing its performance on a retrieve while simultaneously ensuring the other one is sitting patiently with its handler back in the line, exhibiting the steadiness expected of it.

But despite the shortcomings, the system is still encountered and does have the small advantage of requiring one less judge to organize, which can be a difficult enough task.

The Four Judge System

The four judge system is the predominant system used at field trials and the one therefore most likely to be encountered by the trialler. The four judges are arranged in pairs, giving two sets of judges. The judges will decide among themselves how they will be paired for the day, this being discussed before the start of the trial, getting together as soon as they arrive and have been introduced to each other. If there are two 'A' panel judges, they will not judge together, and a non-panel judge is usually paired with the 'A' panel judge. With the pairings decided, they will discuss with the chief steward which 'side' they will take, right or left, with the right-hand pair seeing the odd-numbered dogs in the first round, and the left-hand pair the even-numbered dogs.

Once the judges have seen all their first round dogs, those that are still left in the trial will then have their second round judged by the other judging pair, so those who ran under judges seeing the odd numbers will now run under the pair judging even numbers. If, after the completion of the second round, the judges cannot decide on the final placings, a third round or run-off takes place, with the dogs selected to take part running under all four judges. Each judge in a pair will make an individual assessment of the dog's performance and record it in the judging book independently of the co-judge. They will confer and exchange views throughout the trial, and both will be actively engaged in keeping the trial running as smoothly as possible, often liaising with the other judging pair.

TYPES OF TRIAL

Trials can be walked up, driven or a mixture of both if the nature of the ground permits, so the prospective trialler must be familiar with both methods of game shooting and be prepared for every eventuality. The field trial schedule or programme will probably not give any indication as to the mode of trial, but a call to the field trial secretary beforehand is all that is needed if it is important for you to know.

THE WALKED-UP TRIAL

After the usual preliminaries, the whole trial party moves off to the ground to be used for the first drive. Assuming the four judge system is being employed, the dog steward calls up the first four dogs and makes sure that each handler knows their position in the line, number one on the right of number two and number four on the left of number three, dogs one and two being

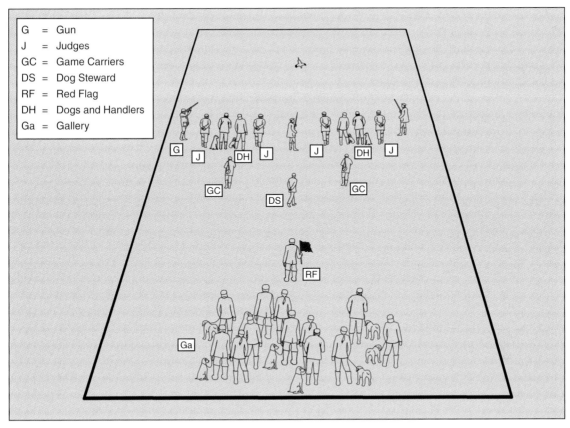

G = Gun
J = Judges
GC = Game Carriers
DS = Dog Steward
RF = Red Flag
DH = Dogs and Handlers
Ga = Gallery

Arrangement of the walked-up trial.

with the right-hand pair of judges. Once the first line is made up, the steward sends them up, on the lead, to the judges who will then make sure that dogs and handlers are correctly positioned: the dogs should be sitting by their handler, lead now off and safely stowed in a pocket. The judges will then position themselves in the line along with the Guns. This constitutes 'the line'.

Also in the line are the game carriers, whose sole task is to collect game from the judges; following on from them are the next dogs to be called up into line behind the red flag, along with the rest of the competitors and any spectators. The chief steward occupies a roving position between the judges and the gallery as circumstances dictate, ensuring that dogs are brought up into the line promptly and the waiting dogs

just behind the line are the correctly numbered ones. If radios are being used, the chief steward will usually stay with the other competitors, sending up the next dog when asked.

At a signal from one of the judges, the whole line moves forwards at a pace dictated either by the steward of the beat (the gamekeeper or landowner) or the judges. Once the line is on the move, the judges will be continuously assessing the heelwork, whether a dog is maintaining the proper heel position relative to the handler, or whether it is forging ahead and needing verbal correction from the handler to bring it back to where it should be. During a walked-up trial, a dog is expected to walk to heel, stopping and sitting when the line stops, walking again to heel when the handler moves on with the line as it advances once more. This should happen without any commands from the handler, although novice dogs may need the occasional reminder, and the judges will take a dim view of repeated commands to 'sit' or 'heel'.

Remember that a single Gun out with his dog for a day's shooting cannot concentrate on shooting while a part of his mind is occupied worrying about what the dog is up to, or might be up to. This is how it would be expected to work on a normal shoot day, and is how the judges will assess performance during the trial.

As the line progresses any birds brought to wing can be tried for by the Guns, and any shot by them will cause the line to halt, when it will be decided whether any have indeed been shot, the number, the point of fall – where they are located – and whether any were seen to be runners. A runner, of course, must be dealt with first, and a judge will send a dog to try for it as quickly as possible. In the first round of retrieving, any birds down will normally be tried for by dogs under the judges nearest to the fall – so a bird shot on the left-hand side of the line, whether in front of or behind the line, will be retrieved by one of the dogs under the judging pair on that side. Game falling in the middle of the line will generally be tried for by the side from which the bird took wing.

Judges can offer a retrieve to the other side at any time, particularly when they have sufficient retrieves for their dogs currently in line and when any 'spare' retrieves could be useful to the others. Another case is when the two dogs running under one of the judging pairs have both failed a retrieve, in which case the other judging pair will come across with their two dogs to try for it. In subsequent retrieving rounds it is usual for cross-retrieving to be employed, especially in All-Aged and Open stakes. Here, a bird shot on the right-hand side of the line will be tried for by one of the dogs under the left-hand judging pair, and vice versa for a bird falling on the left. Such retrieves are more challenging, not only because the distance will be much greater, but a dog right on the end of the line will probably not be in a position to see or mark the fall of a bird at the other end, requiring a blind retrieve to be made.

Once all the retrieves have been collected (or deputed to the picking-up dog) the line can set off again. How the line is made up as the trial progresses is described next.

The Dog Steward

The job of the dog steward with the gallery is to ensure that the correct dogs are up in line with the judges. We have already seen that dogs one to four have been sent up to the line, with the lowest on the right. The next dogs, five and possibly six, are often kept just behind the line but in the centre so they can be quickly up in line when the time arises, minimizing any delay in keeping the trial flowing. Dog five will be sent up to replace the first dog that comes back from the line, let's say dog three: the handler is seen by the dog steward to have put the lead on the dog – a sure sign that the judges have finished with it for now – and invites the handler of number five dog to go up to take the place of dog three in the line.

Dog three and handler will make their way back to the gallery – the dog steward may enquire if the handler is still 'in' or not, as it enables him to make an appropriate note: thus if dog three has been eliminated, he can put an 'X' through the number three and need not worry about that number again. If the handler believes he's still in, then the dog steward now puts another mark against the number three. Sometimes the judges just say 'thank you handler', or 'pick up please, handler', which means the judges have finished with that dog for now, but they don't always explicitly indicate whether the dog is still in the trial. Unless the dog steward knows for a fact that a dog has been eliminated, it must be assumed that it is still in.

Every dog steward will have their own

method of keeping track of who has been where, and where they have to go next, there being no standard notation; thus the following examples may not be how a particular society or individual works, and are given only to illustrate the process:

L   R
③ 4 5   1 2

Here, we can see that dogs one and two are up with the right-hand judging pair, and that dogs three and four have been up with the left-hand pair; and we also know that dog three has now come back from the line, with number five taking its place. As it is not clear whether three has been eliminated or not, a circle is put around the number to indicate that this dog has run and should be sent to run under the right-hand judging pair when the time comes.

Now, dog four is seen to come back from the line, and so the dog steward immediately sends number six forward. On the way back, the handler passes the steward and informs him that he is out, so an 'X' can be put through number four and not considered further. The dog steward will now signal for the next two dogs to come forward to replace those that have gone up to the line. Now the steward's card looks like this:

L   R
③ ✗ 5 6   1 2

So why haven't any dogs been sent to the right-hand judges? Usually the reason is simply that game has been shot on the left-hand side of the line, giving those dogs the chance of retrieves. If the situation continues like this the left-hand judges will start to offer retrieves to the right in order to keep the trial balanced. Luckily, things now start happening on the right, and number one dog comes back – still in the trial – and number seven is sent forward. The card looks like this:

L   R
③ ✗ 5 6   ① 2 7

The trial continues until eventually the following situation is arrived at:

L   R
③ ✗ ⑤ ⑥ ⑨ ✗   ① ✗ ⑦ ✗ ✗ ✗

All twelve dogs have now run, so the first round is concluded. The judges will now confer so as to reach an agreement as to which of the dogs not eliminated should be seen in a second round. Even though a particular dog has done its retrieves and not been eliminated, this does not mean automatic progression to the next round. First the judges must compare their scoring and notes for each dog, and decide whether it has performed sufficiently well to enable them to allow it through. A dog which has had both its retrieves marked as 'B' by both the judges may well find itself not competing in the second round. Ultimately, of course, the decision rests solely at the discretion of the judges.

Continuing with this example, the judges now confirm to the dog steward that they wish to see dogs one, three, five, six, seven and nine in the second round. The steward will inform the competitors of the dogs to be seen in the next round, and will call the second round dogs forward. The first round dogs now need to run under other judges, so by inspection, the dog steward can see that dogs three, five, six and nine need to run under the right-hand judges, and dogs one and seven under the left-hand judges. So getting the second round underway, the line is made up like this:

L   R
7 1   5 3

It is apparent that the left-hand judges only have two dogs – one and seven – to judge, while the right-hand side has four; in an ideal world both sides would have the same number, but things are rarely ideal, even in the world of field trials, and so once dogs one and seven have completed their retrieves (or been eliminated) the right-hand pair continue on their own until all the dogs have been seen – the dog steward's task now reduced to sending up six and nine to the right-hand judges.

This is by no means a universal system, and most field trial secretaries, or those who take on the task of dog steward, have developed their own system which works for them. Experience has shown that while a different coloured pen for each pair of judges would seem to be a good idea from the point of view of clarity, the reality is very different while trying to juggle the two in the cold, pouring rain, dropping one which disappears forever in the undergrowth. Rain is the bane of field trial secretaries and judges alike: pens won't write, pencils smear, the dog steward's list gets progressively wetter and practically illegible, pages of the judges' books get stuck together, ink runs and the drip from the

hat or cap always seems to land right in the middle of the page – always.

THE DRIVEN TRIAL

The driven trial version of a trial is probably more familiar to those who shoot, as it is likely to be how the local shoot operates. In the context of a field trial, it requires the host ground to provide the beating team, including their dogs, and a team of Guns numbering about six. The Guns are usually happy to pay for a day's shooting, which can offset considerably the cost of staging the trial to the promoting society.

There will be a nominated dog steward, often the field trial secretary or the person deputed by the society to run the trial, who is responsible for ensuring that the correct dogs are with the right judges at the right time, so as little time as possible is wasted in getting dogs up into the line as soon as they are required. There will be at least

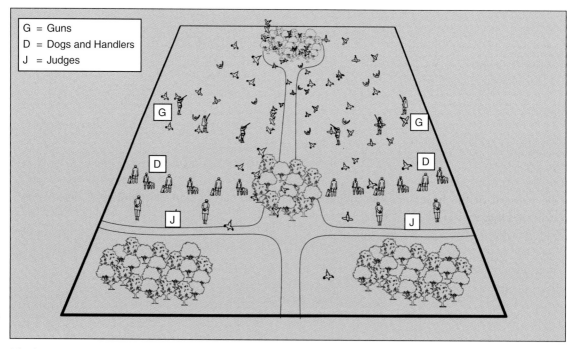

The driven trial.

It's not always pheasant and partridge.

one picking-up dog, whose task is to search for wounded game that cannot be dealt with by those dogs competing in the trial itself – for example, a pricked bird which has set its wings and glided for a considerable distance, too far for any of the trial dogs to attempt to retrieve. A number of spotters are employed whose job is to mark down the position of fallen game.

The beaters start their work at the signal from the steward of the beat once the judges have indicated that they are ready to start: this could be a whistle, a shout or more frequently nowadays by radio, with the steward of the beat in constant contact with the head beater. As the beaters, with their dogs, move their line forwards, birds taking to wing will now start to appear over the Guns, and the action starts. If too many birds are coming over, the steward of the beat may tell the beaters to hold the line for

a while before setting off again, to give the Guns a chance to reload.

A drive may well result in excess of fifty birds on the ground, all of which will need to be retrieved. In the course of a normal shooting day they would be collected either by the Gun's own dog on the peg or by the picking-up team waiting behind the Guns, and these may be supplemented by the dogs in the beating team, who may help in sweeping up at the end of the drive. On a field trial these birds provide the retrieving opportunities on which the competing dogs will be judged, each dog being sent for a particular bird identified by the judges and communicated by them to the handler. The judges therefore need to know the position of every bird fairly accurately in order to tell the handler where to send his dog.

Furthermore every bird will need to be

accounted for and picked up by competing dogs, so it is imperative that all the falls are recorded accurately – and if a large number of birds has been shot, as is often the case, it is very difficult, if not impossible, for the judges alone to recall where they all fell. So the spotters, armed with pen or pencil and some sheets of paper, note the position of a bird as it falls, and mark it with a dot or x on their sheet. At the end of the drive, the spotters' charts are available to the judges to assist them in allocating retrieves.

How the judges position themselves will be dictated by the terrain, but in general terms they will be separated by about thirty to fifty yards, each pair being able to communicate easily with the other judging pair, to ensure the best use of game – a retrieve which is of little value to one pair of judges may well be offered to the judges on the other side. Dogs are sent up to the judges

by the dog steward in exactly the same manner as described above in the walked-up trial, and accounted for in the same way.

In exceptional cases it may be necessary for the judging pairs to be quite some distance apart – for example, in neighbouring fields separated by a hedge. In this case they may take the decision to split the competitors, with one judging pair taking dogs one to six into one of the fields, and the other pair taking the remainder to the other field. Remembering that every dog (if it is still in the trial) must be run under both pairs of judges, in the simplest case dogs one to six and seven to twelve could simply swap judges on the next drive; but the simplest case rarely, if ever, occurs, and it is up to the judges and the steward to keep track of which dog has been under which judge, taking eliminations into account. The trial could also be split into odd and even numbers.

Dogs must be steady off the lead at all times.

Steadiness Drive

Often the first drive of the day will be a steadiness drive, the purpose of which, as the name suggests, is to assess the steadiness of the competing dogs as game is shot around them. All competing dogs are called up and arranged behind the line of Guns in a single long line with the judges so positioned as to afford them a good view of all the dogs in the line. During the drive, birds are driven over the line of Guns by the beaters, and as the birds fall the dogs are expected to remain sitting, off the lead at their handler's side, marking the falls but remaining in position. This can be quite a test, especially as many birds are likely to fall, and some probably very close to a dog, thereby providing a strong temptation. Any dog which 'runs in' – that is, takes it upon itself to go and fetch a fallen bird without being commanded by its handler to do so – will be eliminated from the trial, and will not be permitted to take any further part in it.

The judges will be watching the line for any sign of unsteadiness, and while it is easy to identify (and eliminate) those dogs that have very obviously run in, assessment of other behaviour has to be made; thus a dog shuffling surreptitiously forward of its handler, while not exactly running in, is not being entirely steady either, as is one which is obviously straining to contain itself by leaning further and further forward – although it is not actually moving from its spot, it is on the edge of going for it. Similarly, a dog which makes a move to run in but is brought under quick control by the handler may be excused, but this will be noted by the judges and it will affect its overall placing if at the conclusion of the trial it is being considered for an award. At a Novice

The judges indicate the area of a blind retrieve.

43

stake some leniency can be expected from the judges, but at All-Aged or Open stakes no such allowance will be made.

After the Drive – Retrieving

Once the judges have their first dogs ready to go, they will consult with the spotter(s) to see where the retrieves have been plotted, and decide on their approach to ensure that they are all picked up. A consequence of moving the dogs from where they were sitting is that any marks they had retained may be lost, but in any case the judges will decide which retrieve the dog should be sent for, which could well be one that the dog hadn't marked. Some retrieves will be 'seen' – the bird to be retrieved is in view of the handler – others 'blind' – where the retrieve cannot be seen by the handler – and will be of varying distances. It is largely a matter of luck which

retrieve a dog and handler will be asked to try for when they are called up by the judges.

One of the judges will indicate the retrieve to be performed: in the case of a 'seen' retrieve the bird required will be pointed out to the handler, who must, if in doubt, make sure that the one required by the judge is the same one that the handler thinks is being pointed out. It cannot be emphasized enough how important this is, because picking the wrong bird is an eliminating fault, even if this is due to a genuine misunderstanding between judge and handler – it will be the handler and dog at fault if the wrong retrieve is made, so make absolutely sure with the judge. In the case of an unseen, 'blind' retrieve the judge will either point out the exact location, or a general area in which it is believed the retrieve will be found.

Once the retrieve, or mark, has been established, it's now up to you. Don't feel pressured

The retrieve must be handed immediately to one of the judges.

Directing the dog to a blind retrieve.

into rushing things, but assess in your own mind how the retrieve should be best approached, and do then take your time to set up the dog correctly: the whistle should be in your mouth, make sure the body of the dog is aligned in the direction of the retrieve, and that the dog is paying attention to you and is not distracted by something else – then indicate the direction with an outstretched hand and set the dog off on its way. A tender delivery to hand is expected, and is a basic requirement in the field trial regulations: the dog simply dropping its retrieve in front of the handler does not go down well with the judges.

The retrieve must be handed immediately to one of the judges who will check the bird for damage, evidence of hard mouth, or any other damage caused by the dog. Both judges will check the bird very carefully: a damaged bird is

GAME-FINDING AND HUNTING ABILITY

Game-finding is the ability of the dog, using all its senses and experience, to locate the retrieve, and is considered to be of the highest importance. Some handlers, however, prefer to take the initiative away from the dog and direct it by whistle and hand signal alone; these are usually the professional handlers who have found that on balance this strategy over the course of a number of trials will lead to a better placing or a win. But this insistence on control can also be their downfall, because if the retrieve is not where the handler thinks it is and they persist in directing the dog to that point, even when the dog is trying to go elsewhere, pulled by instinct, they risk not making the retrieve at all. In this instance, had they recognized that the dog knew better and let it use its natural instincts, all would have been well.

Dogs trained in this way will constantly look to the handler for direction, and where the retrieve is well out of sight, and the handler is unable to direct the dog, this method is distinctly disadvantageous. The old adage 'trust your dog' still holds good today, and a dog which is used to working largely on its own, with minimal or no input from the handler, and which learns to trust its instincts and innate ability, by continued success becomes capable of producing the very best that its breeding has instilled.

grounds for elimination from the trial, so if there is any suspicion of damage it will be investigated.

Judging the Retrieve

The judges are looking for the most efficient retrieve, the dog that takes a fast, straight line (as much as the terrain allows) to the point of fall, a quick and unfussy pick-up, a fast return in a straight line, with a tender delivery to hand to finish it off. The game-finding ability of the dog is paramount, and a dog exhibiting superior qualities on the day will be placed above other dogs. The judges' assessment of a dog starts when the lead is taken off and finishes when it is placed back on, and anything in between is under scrutiny.

A seen retrieve, where the dog has seen the fall of the bird, will test the dog's ability to mark the point of fall accurately, even at a great distance, and to quickly make its way to the area of the fall, which it should then hunt with purpose and drive until it finds the scent which enables it to home in on the fall. The handler's method is not assessed by the judges, but they are interested and concerned with the dynamics of the partnership between the dog and its handler. Is there an understanding between them, does the dog trust the handler when he intervenes? Does the handler help the dog? They must assess the handler's delicacy of decision between leaving the dog in peace to do its job, and his prudently judged intervention, only helping when the dog needs some help, which it readily accepts in the knowledge that it will lead to success.

This is at its most evident with the blind retrieve – where the dog has not had the oppor-

Judges assess all aspects of the retrieve.

A judge makes up his notes.

tunity to mark the fall – and is the ultimate test of the partnership. Noisy handling, character-ized by repeated yelling at a distant (or even not so distant!) dog and over-use of the whistle, will be noted by the judge as it constitutes a major fault, and will have a negative impact on the overall assessment made by the judge.

Each judge will assign a letter to the retrieve as they have assessed it, using the grading letters A, B and C, with plus (+) and minus (–) marks to differentiate performance further. Although a judge will use their own system of scoring, it is generally accepted that a dog will start off on a retrieve with an 'A' score, which, if it performed its task faultlessly, it would retain and which would be so entered in the judges' book at the end of its run. Any deviation from the perfect would result in the mark being downgraded, and cumulative errors in the performance would incur further loss of grades, the final

grade given by the judge being an assessment of the overall performance, taking into account all the relevant factors. As we have seen in the walked-up trial above, those dogs with less than an A– grade in the first round would generally be unlikely to progress to the second.

Retrieving Rounds

The usual procedure is for two retrieves to be completed in the first round and one in the second. But what do we mean by 'retrieving round'? A retrieving round is completed when all the dogs eligible for the round have completed the two retrieves under one of the judging pairs. When the first round has been completed, the judges come together and confer in order to arrive at the list of dogs that will compete in the second round. Clearly, any dogs already eliminated can be discounted. As each

Ready for the run-off.

judging pair has seen every dog complete two retrieves, and each judge makes their own notes, there will be a set of four separate notes on each and every dog's performance. These notes form the basis of the conference as the judges go through each dog individually, comparing the marks they have given.

Usually, dogs with less than an A– grade would not be expected to progress to the second round, and those with an A– grade could be on sticky ground if the general standard of the other dogs in the trial is much higher – so for example if there were six dogs with A+ and A grades, these would be candidates for the second round over those scoring A–.

Conference over, the judges will now have arrived at a list of the dogs they would like to see compete in the second round; this list is given to the chief steward, who will call all the competi-

tors together to announce the list. The second round proceeds as with the first, at the end of which the judges will again confer, comparing their individual scores for each dog, along with

---

DRIVES VERSUS RETRIEVING ROUNDS

A common source of confusion is the number of drives versus retrieving rounds. They are independent of each other. A drive makes retrieves possible, and the first drive of the day will coincide with the first retrieving round, but if the drive yields a relatively small number of birds to retrieve and only half of the competing dogs successfully retrieved them all, then on the next drive, the second, the first retrieving round is still taking place because the remaining dogs from the first drive still have to demonstrate their retrieves. On the other hand, if the first drive yields a great many birds, there may be enough for two retrieving rounds to be completed. Usually, three drives are about the norm for a trial.

the notes they made of performance at the time. This time it may be possible for the judges to separate the dogs sufficiently for them to be able to award the winning places, in which case the trial can be called to an end. However, it may be the case that they cannot agree in separating the top dogs, and a run-off is then instituted as a decider. The chief steward will be informed as to which dogs are required for a run-off.

The Run-off

The run-off may be a seen or a blind retrieve, depending on the level of the stake; the dogs required will be called up into line and sent for the retrieves in the order determined by the judges, which may not be in accordance with the number on their handler's armband. All the judges at the trial will assess the retrieves in the run-off, which will then enable them to place the dogs in the final awards.

The End of the Driven Trial and Awards

The driven trial is formally declared at an end when the judges so declare, or when they inform the chief steward that they no longer require to see any more dogs run. If they have not yet decided upon the final placings, they will now convene in a huddle, calling the chief steward over to receive their decision. The chief steward then informs the competitors that the trial has ended, and the whole field usually returns to the meeting point where the awards ceremony and thank-yous will be carried out.

Drive Certificate

A drive certificate can be issued by two 'A' panel judges to any dog that has demonstrated to their satisfaction that it has sat quietly in line and was steady to shot and fall during the drive. The drive certificate must be gained before a dog can be made up to be a field trial champion, and has no other use, so it is only really relevant to those

The judges confer.

who are close to achieving that goal – that is, dogs which have already won one or two qualifying stakes.

Water Certificate

The water certificate is another piece of documentation that is necessary for a dog to be made up to a field trial champion. To achieve it the dog is required to enter water and swim under the watchful eye of two field trial panel judges, who will need to sign the certificate. Note that there is no requirement to retrieve anything, just to demonstrate the dog's willingness to swim, but a thrown dummy is the easiest way to get the dog into the water, and while steadiness and a nice delivery to hand are to be expected, they do not form part of the test and are not considered by the judge.

It is important to note that as a retriever is not required to complete a water test as part of the trial, many of the trial grounds do not have water available for the purpose – and if they do, it may be some distance away on a completely different part of the ground, and could be a major inconvenience to organize without due notice. For these reasons, if a handler wishes to undertake a water test it is imperative that he contacts the field trial secretary before the trial to ascertain whether water is available and whether a test would be possible.

Both certificates must signed by an 'A' panel judge at the trial, and will be given to the competitor who has requested them at the conclusion of the trial – assuming, of course, that they have been granted. They do not usually form part of the awards presentation proceedings for the winning dogs, and are simply handed to the competitor. The certificate must subsequently be sent to the Kennel Club field trials department.

THE CHAMPIONSHIP

The International Gundog League Retriever Society staged the first championship in 1909, and apart from the war years (and foot and mouth in 1967) has held them every year since. The event is staged over three days at the most prestigious locations, and sees well over fifty of the top performing dogs in the season competing for the ultimate accolade. To be able to enter the championship a dog must qualify to do so, and apart from the current champion, entitled to defend its title, and the current Irish champion, all other dogs must have, as a

The water certificate can be completed at a trial.

minimum, one 'A' qualification and one 'B' or 'C' qualification, or three B qualifications. These are defined as follows:

'A' qualification:	First in an Open (two-day) stake, twenty runners or more
'B' qualification:	Second in an Open (two-day) stake, twenty runners or more First in an Open (one-day) stake, ten runners or more
'C' qualification:	Third or fourth in an Open (two-day) stake, twenty or more runners Second or third in an Open (one-day) stake, ten runners or more

Qualifications must be won at a trial organized by one of the eighty-seven field trial clubs and societies recognized for the championships.

Chapter 3

Spaniel Field Trials

Spaniels were recorded in the UK in 1576 by John Caius. By the early 1800s spaniels from the same litter were being divided by their weight to perform different functions, the heavier ones to 'spring' gamebirds into the air for hawks to kill and retrieve to the handler, and the lighter ones to 'cock', or flush woodcock: these were the forerunners of today's springer and cocker breeds.

These two breeds are the most popular hunting-retriever dogs in the country, and they are admired worldwide, many being exported all over the world, a testament to the excellence of both the breeds. They are enthusiastic hunting

An English springer spaniel waits its turn.

Spaniels are exciting to watch.

dogs, capable of working tirelessly for the whole of the shooting day, and it is at the field trial that this enthusiasm is showcased. Here their amazing drive can still astonish even those who are well acquainted with them, the springer bashing its way through the bracken and frenetically questing amongst the rhododendrons, and the cocker, no less frenetic but being smaller threading its way beneath the bushes and fronds at dizzying speed.

Field trials are held for AV ('Any Variety') Spaniel and separate classes for Cocker, English Springer (ESS), and the rarer breeds such as the Clumber, Field Spaniel or the Sussex – sometimes known as AVNSC: 'Any Variety Spaniel (except English Springer Spaniel) and Spaniel (Cocker)'. Spaniels are expected to quarter the ground in front of the handler, flushing any game they find on their beat, sitting to the flush (or to shot) and retrieving on command. The ideal

quartering pattern is shown in the diagram overleaf, although this is an idealized version and it is unlikely that a spaniel will actually follow this pattern precisely, as the terrain it encounters usually precludes this, especially in woodland; however, it should work in front of the handler, running from side to side in front of him, turning away from him at the end of its beat in order to move its beat line forwards. How far it ranges on each side of the handler is not a prescribed distance, but should be suited to the terrain, and sufficient to cover the ground in front of the Guns positioned to the right and left.

While not as influenced by the wind direction as the pointing breeds, spaniels do change their quartering pattern as the wind direction changes. This is most obviously seen when the wind comes from behind – a back wind – which causes them to run forwards some distance, then

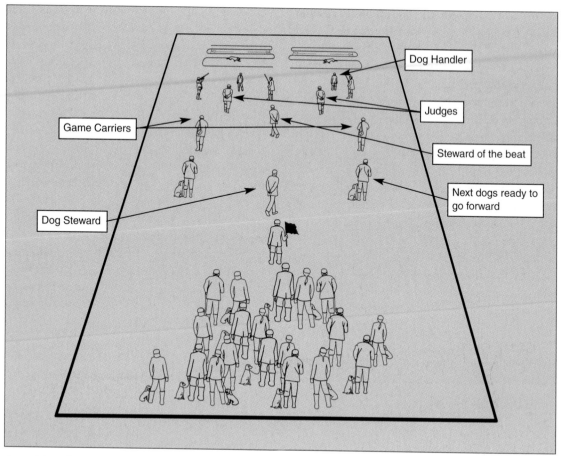

Dog Handler	
Judges	
Steward of the beat	
Next dogs ready to go forward	
Game Carriers	
Dog Steward	

A spaniel trial.

to turn back into the wind and work the ground back towards the handler.

The usual number of dogs that run in a one-day stake is sixteen, the relatively large number being managed by running two dogs at the same time, which, as we have just seen, is made possible by virtue of the fact that the length of the beat is quite small compared to the other hunting breeds. The judges will position the handlers so that the distance between them is judged to be such that the dogs won't overlap at the extremity of their beats: ideally the right-hand end of the beat of the dog running on the left-hand side will just touch that of the left-hand extremity of the dog running on the right, so that the whole length of the beat of the two

together will be covered and no game left missed somewhere along the line.

In practice this seems to work remarkably well, although occasionally a dog will stray further than it should into the beat of the other, in which case the handler should pip it back with the whistle to re-establish its beat once more. While some youngsters can get caught up with each other, with one or the other finding it a great game to chase the other one around, in the main, and particularly with older and more experienced dogs, they are so concentrated on their own task that they are virtually oblivious to the presence of the others. Watch the beating line on your local shoot and you'll see the same thing, with as many spaniels as can be mustered on the day making up the line all busily rushing about their business without any regard for the others.

There is a risk here for you and your aspiring field trial dog in that while you have trained your dog to sit to flush and to shot and may even have encouraged it to pause momentarily, acknowledging the presence of game before flushing it into the air, the average shoot dog will have had no such training. It will simply keep going, which, when this occurs at every flush and shot, may well have the very undesirable effect of undoing the good training you have instilled into your own dog.

Many 'serious' triallers do not allow their dogs to mix in with this uncouth rabble for fear of compromising the hard-won behaviour that will hopefully win them a field trial, and will only run them either exclusively in trials – and there are enough of these for that option to be very realistic – or on a shoot with other similarly trained dogs. But many wish to enjoy their working dog both on the local shoot and in trials, and why not? It is often said that 'if the dog does a good job in the shooting field, then it will make a good field trial dog'.

Spaniel trials are exciting – the dogs see to that, because the sheer speed at which they work means there is never a dull moment. Unfortunately for the gallery, which of course includes spectators as well as competitors impatiently waiting their turn, all the action takes place up front and is often not visible, particularly in woodland. And here is a tip: to get up to the action, be a game carrier! The game carrier is positioned right behind the judge, and this is

Quartering at speed, a young cocker spaniel.

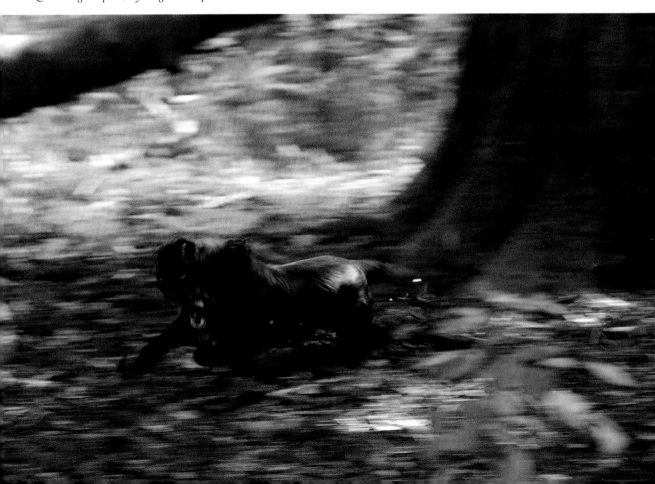

the best seat in the house to see what's going on, to observe not only the dogs but also how the trial is conducted. Make a polite call to the field trial secretary to offer your services, and the chances are that they will take you on.

ON THE DAY

Having gained a run in a field trial, the lucky entrant arrives expectantly in good time to get the armband and running order and to listen to the usual preliminaries, introductions and notices for the day.

In the main, spaniel trials are conducted in more or less open woodland, but with plenty of bracken cover of varying density. There are two judges, each judging one dog running in front of them: thus two dogs run simultaneously, with handlers and judges so spaced that the beat of each dog does not overlap or interfere with the other. There are two Guns positioned to the left and right of each dog, more or less defining the width of the beat, and this constitutes the 'line'. Following a short distance behind each judge is a game carrier, whose function is, as the name suggests, to relieve the judge of the retrieved game. Further behind is the 'gallery' – competitors waiting to be called up into line, and any spectators, all of whom should be behind the red flag.

While this is the usual arrangement, when rabbit is the primary quarry the steward of the beat may ask for the game carriers, a dog steward and the next dogs waiting to come up into the line to be as close as possible to the line in order that the Guns can take ground shots behind the line safely. The gallery may also be repositioned to one side of the beat.

The chief steward's main job in the body of the trial is to act as dog steward, to ensure that the next dog to run is ready to go forward, and this requires some experience and concentration. While it might seem simple enough to get the next dog ready, in reality it can be more complicated than one might think, because each judge needs to be fed with the next correctly numbered dog, odd or even, and the steward must make sure that as a dog returns from its run another one is sent up to the line immediately.

The steward of the beat is the shoot's game-keeper or his nominated representative, occasionally the land or shoot owner, who will direct the judges as to the ground that is to be covered next, in which direction. The whole trial is dependent on finding game, and therefore to a great degree dependent on the steward of the beat taking it to where he believes game will be found.

Dogs are divided equally between the judges, with odd-numbered dogs – one, three, five, seven, nine, eleven, thirteen, fifteen – running under the judge positioned to the right of the

The trial is dependent upon the steward of the beat finding game.

line, while the other judge has the even-numbered dogs – two, four, six, eight, ten, twelve, fourteen, sixteen). When both the judges have seen their eight dogs, those dogs which have not been eliminated then have a second round, this time running under the other judge. In this way, each judge gets to judge all the dogs. It is the job of the dog steward (often the field trial secretary) to send the right dog up to the right judge, and is a job which requires organization but above all concentration, especially if competitors are running two dogs.

When the steward of the beat has pointed out the ground to be worked and the direction in which the trial should proceed to both judges, they will take up their respective positions and call the first two dogs forward, number one to the right-hand judge and number two to the left-hand judge. To facilitate a faster turnaround of dogs up in the line, dogs three and four will also

be sent forward by the steward to wait a short distance behind the game carrier. Canny handlers make good use of the position: if the dog running has a bird shot your dog might well be in a good position to mark the fall – in dense cover the dog running may see the flush and hear the shot, but not see the fall if it happens to be below the level of cover or otherwise disadvantaged. Your dog may also be similarly disadvantaged, but it may not, and may have had a clear sighting of the fall, which is a big advantage. The running dog will be sent for the retrieve, but if it fails, the retrieve will be offered to the judge on the other side. If this dog makes the retrieve successfully, the first dog (known as the first dog down) will be eliminated, as its eye will have been wiped (an eye-wipe).

However, if the second dog also fails the judges will normally go forward and search the area of the fall. If they find it, it will be held aloft

Rabbit is often the primary quarry.

for all to see and both dogs that had failed are now eliminated. The judges can try more dogs if they see fit, but it is not usual practice to try more than two.

For completeness, let us go back to the point where the retrieve was offered to the other judge. There is no obligation for this judge to accept, and although very unlikely, there can be circumstances when it might be refused: it could be that the dog running under the judge was not steady to the shot and had thereby just eliminated itself, and was therefore not eligible to undertake the retrieve. Or it could be that the dog had already made retrieves and was just coming to the end of its run, in which case giving this dog the retrieve would be a waste of game, particularly if game were short and the retrieve would be much appreciated by the next dog.

Now the handler waiting patiently behind the judge on the left will be called up into line to take on the retrieve, and if he has been keeping up close to the action, the dog might have had the distinct advantage of having been able to mark the fall. Although the act of moving forward to the judge will change the picture that the dog has seen of the fall, in that it will be sent from a different position from that in which it saw it, there will still be a big advantage.

The message, then, is clear: as the next dog up in line, get as close as you can, even to the extent of being told to back off a little by the judge. As one judge put it: 'If you haven't been told to back off, you aren't close enough!'

It can happen that one side of the trial has less game than the other and so takes much longer to run through the card, while the judge who has more available game runs through his first set of dogs relatively quickly and so can make a start on judging those dogs which have run under the other judge. If the game situation remains the

Nervously waiting to be called up to the line.

Delivering a partridge to hand.

same, this judge is now still going through dogs faster than the one on the other side, with the result that he now runs out of dogs and has to wait for dogs to finish running under the other judge before they are available to him.

This has the highly undesirable consequence that a dog that has just completed its run under the first judge, is now expected to go over and run immediately under the second judge. Clearly this dog is at a huge disadvantage, having had little time to recover from its run before being expected to do it all over again. Usually the waiting judge will give the dog a few minutes rest before calling it forward, but even so, it is still at a disadvantage, especially as it is highly likely that it has just had to run for much longer because of the lack of game. On the up side, if the game situation has remained the same on the side to which it has now come, it should mean

that it will not have to run for very long before it has a find and a retrieve. Unfortunately there is no satisfactory solution to this situation, and handlers understand that this is just something that can happen, frustrating as it may be.

THE RUN

The judge calls for the first or 'next dog', greeting the handler with a handshake. The position of the Guns on each side is pointed out, and this is usually the width of the dog's beat – it is expected to work the ground in front of it, ranging out on each side of the handler as far as the Guns on each side. The judge will also indicate the direction in which the handler is to go. This done, the judge will wish the handler good luck, which is the signal for him to cast the dog off. The more experienced handler will already have taken in the judge's brief, as well as quickly assessing the ground given for the run.

Covering your Ground

The judges will always place the highest importance on the game-finding ability of the dog, and to find game, the dog must cover the ground thoroughly, the handler overseeing its work and directing it where necessary. Not covering ground can result in game being missed, and if a bird does get up from a piece of ground that the dog should have covered, and the judge notices it, the dog will be eliminated from the trial – the handler will be asked to 'pick up' the dog, recall it and put the lead on – a cursory 'bad luck' from the judge and that is your trial over.

It is therefore paramount that you, as the handler, make every effort to see that the dog is ranging out as far as the Guns on each side, and to make sure that any bushes or brashings on the dog's beat are thoroughly investigated. If the dog doesn't do it by itself, then you need to make sure that you direct it to do so.

On finding game, the dog is expected to flush it immediately into the air, but once the bird has left the ground the dog should sit and watch it fly away, or, in the case of a rabbit, sit to the flush. The Guns are now the key element to come into play and will hopefully promptly be able to kill the bird or ground game stone dead. At the sound of the shot, the whole line comes to a halt, and that includes the dog running under the other judge – it is expected to sit to shot and wait for the next command.

The dog that flushed the quarry should now be sitting, waiting expectantly for a signal from

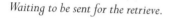

Waiting to be sent for the retrieve.

its handler. When the judge is satisfied that the dog is steady to the shot and the fall he will direct the handler to 'send your dog'. Don't just send the dog: wait for the judge to tell you. On open ground the dog may well have marked the point of fall, and on being sent should have no difficulty in locating the fall and retrieving it promptly to hand. But particularly in woodland with much bracken, and with the dog's eye level being just a few inches above the ground, it is unlikely that it will have been able to see the fall of a bird, much less a rabbit already at ground level, although it may have heard the crash as the bird hit the ground and have some idea of the direction from this sound.

In any event it is a blind retrieve, and the handler will be given a mark by the judge and then asked to send the dog for it. In this case, some handling will be necessary to direct the dog to the point of fall, but the less interference from the handler the better, and the least intervention will count positively in the eye of the judge – and of course, the most important thing is for the retrieve to be successful. Delivery tenderly to hand is essential.

As always in a field trial, the retrieve must be immediately handed to the judge who will check for signs of hard mouth (if the game has been damaged). Assuming everything is satisfactory, the judge, having handed the retrieve to the waiting game-carrier, will ask the handler either to hunt the dog on, or, if satisfied by the work that has been demonstrated, to pick the dog up, signalling the end of that particular run. The handler should retire back towards the gallery and chief steward. The judge, having made appropriate notes on the run in his judging book, will then call the next dog, waiting patiently at a discreet distance, up to the line.

Failed Retrieve

If the dog is unable to find the retrieve for whatever reason, one of the judging pair will call across to that on the other side to offer him the retrieve first. If this dog is successful it will have 'wiped the eye' of the previous dog, which is now eliminated from the trial. If, however, this dog is also unsuccessful the judge will ask the handler to recall the dog and put it on the lead. Both pairs of judges will now go forward and search the area and if they find the retrieve both dogs tried are eliminated; if they do not, then both dogs may continue in the trial.

The Second Round

When each of the judges has had the eight dogs run under him, those not previously eliminated will now run under the other judge. Both judges will confer with the chief steward, who will take a list from both of them of the numbers of the dogs which should be tried in the second round. Quite often, however, the trial may not stop at all and the second round will just start seamlessly, each judge knowing when they've reached dog number fifteen or sixteen and expecting dog numbers two and one next, respectively. If they don't, it is because that dog has been eliminated on the other side.

In this way, the constraints of time later in the season can be mitigated somewhat, and often judges will have already stated at the beginning of the trial that their intention is to 'run straight through' without a break for lunch, or a very short one 'on the hoof'. This seamless transition does rely on the dog steward being completely on top of the job and having the next dog available for both judges in good time.

In this second round, the judges will be looking out for the possibility of a spare retrieve. It is something of a luxury to have more quarry down than is needed for the two dogs in the line, but it is likely that there are dogs still in the trial who still need a retrieve, for example those which have hunted and flushed but with nothing shot, leaving them without a retrieve. With such a retrieve available, the judges can call up a dog to try it, doing so in strict numerical order.

At the end of the second round, when all the dogs remaining in the trial have been seen by both judges, they will stop and compare their notes to see if they can place dogs in the awards. This conference may well take some time as they go carefully through their notebooks dog by dog discussing the run, the merits and how each assessed the performance. Clearly if many dogs have been eliminated then the conference will be correspondingly shorter. With all the assessments made, they will try to place the dogs in order of merit, and if they can indeed agree on the top placings, then the trial can be ended there and then. If not, a run-off between some, or all, of the top dogs will be required to separate them.

END OF TRIAL

The trial is brought to an end when the judges have agreed they do not wish to see any more dogs run. They will confirm their placings to the chief steward so that the award cards can be made out.

SPANIEL CHAMPIONSHIPS

The English Springer Spaniel Championship (ESS) is an annual event run by the Spaniel Club on behalf of the Kennel Club in January towards the end of the shooting season, thus giving as much time as possible to qualify. The Cocker Spaniel Championship is also held annually

A retrieve may be over water.

under the auspices of the Kennel Club, usually in the middle of January towards the end of the shooting season; details are published in the *Kennel Club Gazette* and on the website, with many of the shooting press also publishing information on working events.

Only qualified dogs are eligible to enter: this includes the previous year's champion who is allowed to defend the title, while others must win a first in an Open stake in the current field trial year. The ESS is run over three days, the Cocker over two, and both events are held in the highest regard, with the best organization and always at stunning, prestigious locations.

Competitors at the Cocker Spaniel Championships 2011 at Drumlanrig Castle. (Photo by kind permission of Nick Ridley)

Chapter 4

HPR Field Trials

The basic format of an HPR field trial consists of twelve dogs which are run singly for about ten minutes one after the other under the direction and watchful eye of two judges accompanied by up to four Guns whose sole task is to shoot game for the dogs to retrieve. The dogs are required to hunt and point any game that is found, must flush the game into the air when directed, remain steady to shot and fall, and finally retrieve the game to hand. Unless eliminated, each dog will have a minimum of two runs, sometimes more if the game situation is poor. Those who have completed the hunt, point and retrieve successfully are invited to complete a final retrieve out of water, and may at the end be the lucky recipients of a field trial award. But as you might expect, it is rarely that simple!

Guns at a trial.

A German wirehaired pointer makes a good retrieve.

ON THE DAY

The first priority is to be on time! It is important to arrive well before the published start of the trial, usually 9am, planning your journey with sufficient leeway in case of accidents, traffic jams and the other 101 things that can make driving a frustrating experience. At most trials, there will be limited space to exercise, so it is a good idea to find somewhere beforehand to let your dog(s) out.

Once the introductions and reserve list of runners has been dealt with, the chief steward will ask the judges to make any opening remarks. They will usually indicate whether ground game is to be shot, whether the Guns will shoot only pointed birds or anything that is a sporting shot within range, and whether birds can be shot on the flank or when a dog is out on a retrieve. These decisions will be based on the

stake being run and the wishes of the game-keeper. In a Novice stake it is usual for only pointed birds to be shot, and often ground game will not be shot. In the second round the instructions to the Guns may well change, especially if retrieves are required. In All-Aged and Open stakes the Guns are usually instructed to shoot anything within range, pointed or not.

When the usual formalities immediately prior to the start of the trial have been completed, the steward will usually call for the first three dogs to come up – the first dog to run will go straight on up to the judges to start immediately, while the steward always has the next two in line up with him following on behind the judges so they can be called up promptly to the line without delay. The rest of the field (the gallery) follows at a safe distance grouped behind the person designated red flag.

For those further down the running order it

The gallery can be very sociable.

is valuable to observe the dogs running in front of you as closely as possible. Take the opportunity to notice the direction of the wind, and do so regularly as it may well change. You will be able to assess the scenting conditions and the amount of game, whether it is plentiful with a dog quickly coming on point, or whether dogs are having to hunt hard to find anything.

SETTING UP YOUR RUN

To be successful in a trial and gain an award the judges must be able to record that a dog can hunt (H), point (P) any game that it finds, and retrieve (R) shot game to command; all three must be shown. The best demonstration of this is the dog that hunts and finds game, points it, and flushes the bird on your command; it must be steady to

the flush, shot and fall of the bird, which it subsequently retrieves.

The judges will be most impressed by the H, P and R that is completed in sequence, and perfectly executed, and this will give you the chance of gaining a good placing in the awards, and even of winning the trial. In reality you may not have the opportunity to complete the sequence in one go: the dog may hunt incredibly well but not find any birds to point; it could find a bird, point and flush it correctly, but the bird is missed by the Guns, so while the 'hunt' and 'point' parts have been accomplished, the dog did not have the opportunity of a retrieve. It may be that you are called up to do a retrieve (perhaps because the dog before you has failed) before you have had the opportunity to run, and success here will mean that you will be credited with the retrieve but still have the hunt and point to complete. The H, P and R can be done in any sequence.

Head wind.

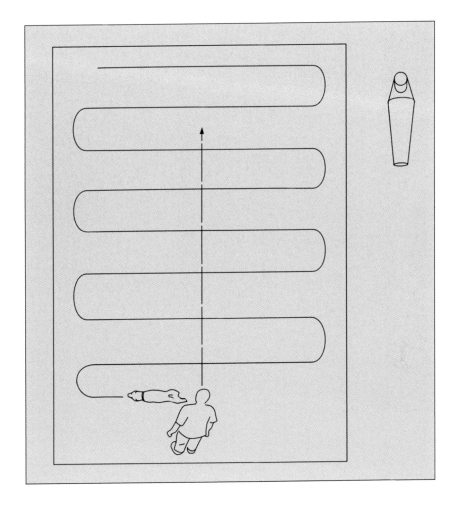

Many handlers new to field trials feel that it is best to have a blank first run, with no excitement, the dog hunting happily but not finding anything. This is down to nerves, however, and the thought of having to deal with a point and retrieve, with all the things that can possibly go wrong, leads them to believe that a quiet first run will give them time to settle down and get used to the idea of running a dog in a trial. This may well be the case, but the down side of this approach is that if the first run is indeed blank, it means there is more pressure on the second run because everything will then need to be demonstrated on that run. The risk here, of course, is that there may well not be the opportunities to get the H, P and R that you need, and

you are risking the outcome on a single attempt. Experienced handlers try and get everything done on the first run, and if something does go wrong, well, that's trialling and there is nothing to say that what went wrong on the first run would not have gone equally awry on the second.

On being sent forward to the judges by the steward, hang back a little if they are still conferring amongst themselves, until they indicate for you to come forward. The judges will check your number and then indicate to you the ground they wish you to cover and the direction to go, and will point out the extent of the beat they wish to see covered, if it is not obvious. They may say to take the Guns on either side as

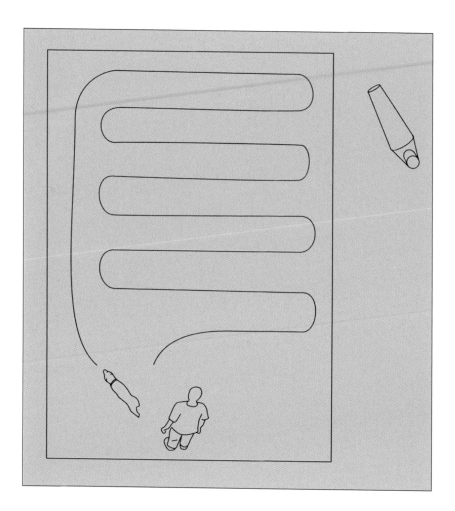

Back wind.

the width of the beat the dog should run (this may be because they want to divide a field up into strips and don't want your dog spoiling the ground that they plan to use for later dogs), or they may simply say 'There's the field, off you go'. If you are not sure what is meant, ask before you set your dog off. It is now up to you to decide how best to manage the beat with regard to the prevailing wind and other considerations, to notice pockets that will need covering, or likely bushes to be checked.

Where's the Wind?

The first thing to do is determine the direction of the prevailing wind. With a stiff breeze it is an easy matter; more problematic is when there is little or no discernible breeze, or it appears to be swirling round. It can help to put a wet finger in the air, or observe the smoke from a cigarette, or from the smoke matches that plumbers and air-conditioning engineers use to detect airflow. Throwing a tuft of grass only works when the wind is sufficiently strong to be able to move them, which is airflow you should be able to detect anyway.

Head Wind
As we have seen, the HPR hunts for game by quartering the ground in front of it, but because the scent it needs to locate game is carried on the wind, the dog has to position itself such that

it has the best chance of catching a whiff of the quarry it is seeking. This is most evidently going to be directly downwind, and so the HPR will automatically adjust its running pattern so that it is at all times running across the face of the oncoming wind. It is easiest for the dog, and the most advantageous, when the wind is a head wind – that is, it is blowing directly into the face of the dog and handler when both are facing the field.

Where at all possible, the dog must be positioned so that it runs into the wind, especially the younger dog. At field trials the judges will do their utmost to ensure that dogs are, whenever possible, run into the wind at every level of field trial stake, although the All-Aged and Open level dogs should be capable of managing wind from any direction.

With the head wind, the handler in the company of the Guns will move up the field in a line behind the quartering dog which is also making its progress directly up the field, maintaining a regular quartering pattern working from side to side running across the oncoming breeze.

Back Wind

Running with a back wind is the least favourable wind direction as scent is being blown away from the dog if it runs with the wind. The second disadvantage is that any noise made by the shooting party will be carried on the wind into the ears of the wary game bird, providing it with a timely early warning of danger approaching, thereby enabling it to make the very sensible decision to run away.

To counter the problem of the scent drifting with the wind away from its nose, the HPR adopts a different running strategy: first it will run out downwind away from you in a straight line until it is some distance away (200 yards or so), before turning to run across the wind and to start quartering, with the wind blowing directly towards it – that is, it now has a head wind, and will work its way back up towards you.

Dogs vary in their ability to work a back wind in the textbook fashion described above, and as shown in the diagram, some may indeed be incapable of making a good job of it, while others can execute it perfectly. Those less able can usually be improved through training.

Cheek Wind

As the name suggests, a cheek wind may be felt on either one of the cheeks and denotes a wind that blows at an angle to your face, round to 90 degrees (when it would be blowing on one or the other side of the face). From the diagram you can see the dog has altered its quartering pattern so that it is now running along a line that is at a slant to the original pattern in order to be still running across the face of the wind. While the dog happily continues on its way it is unaware that it is now running a longer beat than previously, but we need to consider what happens when the handler turns to walk directly into the wind to follow the dog. He would now be heading to a point some way short of the end of the field, which is not where he wants to end up, and also, by doing so, he would no longer be walking in the middle of the dog's beat.

Continuing on this line, one side of the dog's beat will be getting shorter and shorter until eventually there is nowhere to run. This would not be good. Furthermore, the handler is now at the upwind edge and in the worst possible place to continue. The solution is for the handler, as soon as the cheek wind is noticed, to move towards the downwind edge of the field and walk along that. It may be a good idea to walk a short quartering pattern so the dog does not notice any difference in your movements compared to those it would normally expect.

For the beginner, the cheek wind is often a difficult thing to come to terms with, especially if the wind changes in the middle of the run. If you are faced with a cheek wind from the very start, take extra time to work out how you are going to approach the run – how the dog will run, and where you should be walking – and do

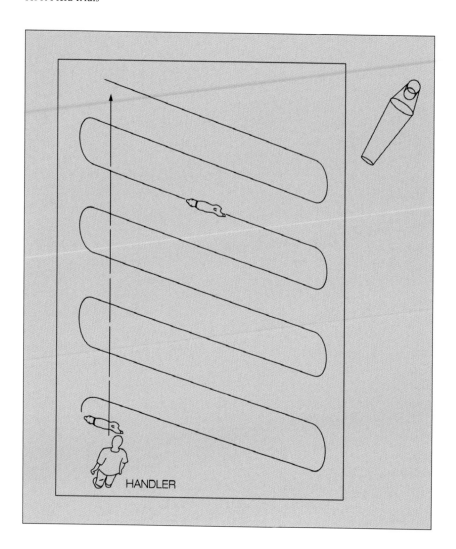

Cheek wind.

remember to cast the dog off in the direction that will give it the longest run. And as noted before, don't move forwards until the dog has crossed in front of you, ensuring the ground you are about to step into has been covered. Take some comfort from the fact that it's only you with the difficulty: the dog will just get on with it.

Changing Wind

You should now have the idea that keeping tabs on what the wind is doing is important, not only at the beginning of the run when you take the time to work out where it is and how best to manage it, but also during the run itself. Once you've started, it is all too easy to forget about the wind as you get involved with watching the dog, managing the run to ensure good ground coverage, perhaps intervening to get a likely bush investigated, while watching where you are going. Furthermore, as you move forwards you create your own impression of wind – if you run forward when it's dead calm you will feel wind pressure on your face – your movement will give rise to your sensing the apparent wind direction, which may well be different to the actual wind direction.

As we have seen, the dog will adjust its

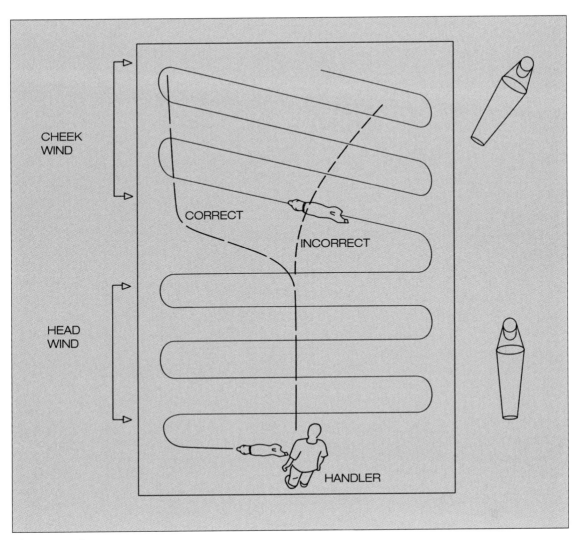

CHEEK WIND

HEAD WIND

CORRECT

INCORRECT

HANDLER

Changing wind.

hunting pattern according to the wind, so the best indicator of what is happening is to observe how it is moving to see if the angle of the pattern in relation to you has changed. This may not always be easy to see or work out, but simply standing still for a couple of moments is an easy way to check. Do remember though, that what you feel on your face may well be different to what is happening down at the height of the dog's nose.

MANAGING THE GROUND

When you are called up to start your run, first sit the dog and remove the lead. Take a moment to check the direction of the wind and decide which way to cast the dog off and how you propose to work the beat given. It is easy for a beginner to forget all this in the excitement of being there, but it is important to take the time to do the basics. More experienced handlers will have checked out the beat and the wind on the way up to the judges, and will already have planned how to start their run. Try and do the same.

Once you have cast your dog off, do not move forwards at once, but wait until the dog has gone past you in front before advancing. The reason is this: if you move forwards immediately, you are moving into ground that has not yet been covered by the dog, and when it turns to come back past you, your forward movement will cause it to take a line further forward than it would have done had you stood still. You have therefore created an area of ground that will not be covered by the dog but which could well still contain game. If game gets up from this ground the judges will terminate your run and the dog will be eliminated for missing game. You will not be comforted by the knowledge that this was caused by your error and not the poor dog, and it is a classic beginner's error.

Faced with starting at the very edge of a field,

Don't move forwards immediately.

it is a good plan to stand well back from the edge before casting off the dog to ensure that it has a chance to run along the edge and thereby cover this ground before advancing into the field proper. If you are running on a back wind, then you won't be moving forwards anyway, so it is less of a problem in this respect.

Different types of ground – root crops, game cover crops, woodland, hedges – will also dictate how you manage your run.

Sugar Beet and Root Crops

Sugar beet is a fine crop in which to run an HPR, but by no means the easiest, particularly for the younger or inexperienced dog. The large field sizes give ample opportunity to see the dogs ranging wide, which is all too rare nowadays and a real treat for all. It is hard going for the dog (and for the human!) and the leaf cover provides

the game bird with fantastic opportunities to run ahead unseen and to double back behind the line of the quartering dog. The dog makes a great deal of noise crashing through the crop, providing a terrific early warning to anything in front, which only encourages them to run on forwards. Furthermore the noise makes it more difficult for the dog to hear your whistle, some taking this as the perfect excuse not to listen! But for the dog that runs well and can keep up with the game sufficiently for it to stop running, crouching down to conceal itself gives the dog the perfect opportunity to point and hold the birds fast.

Game Cover

Most shoots grow some kind of game cover to feed and hold their birds, and these crops are very often encountered in trials. The up side is

Root crops can be hard work!

that there is a good chance of finding birds in them, the down side is that there may well be too many! In addition, early on in the season the crop may well be thick and high, making it very difficult to see what your dog is up to. Later on, when the cover becomes thinner, game crops can be the perfect ground on which to run. The watchword in higher and thicker game crops is cover your ground: don't let the dog run on forwards unchecked, make sure that it is working the ground to left and right, and keep it working as close to you as possible. Use the whistle if you have to – judges appreciate quiet handling, but given the choice between a judge's appreciation and being eliminated from the trial because you didn't keep your dog under control and covering its ground, the choice is clear: use the whistle.

It is worth remembering that the judges can only judge the dog on what they can actually see, so working under these conditions can work for you (the dog does something wrong, but gets away with it as it out of sight), or against you (your dog actually does some wonderful work which goes unseen and cannot be credited).

If the dog just runs straight in front of you down to the end, flushing birds all over the place, you have not only ruined your own chances of succeeding in the trial, but also the chances of those behind you. Proceed with caution, working the dog methodically down the strip, making sure the edges are covered. This is particularly important if the game cover has a hedge line on one side – it is essential to get your dog to check the hedge regularly, because if you don't, you run the double risk of missing a bird and being eliminated by the judges for not covering your ground.

Slow down as you approach the end. Any birds pushed forwards will be waiting until the very last moment before flying, so you actually have the best chance of your dog being able to hold a bird on point if you are very careful that any of the other birds are not frightened into the air by its, or your, approach. Be aware, too, that when

you get your dog to flush the bird it is pointing, this may well result in any number of others being flushed at the same time, and the resulting volley of fire from the expectant Guns, coupled with the flurry of flushing birds, may all be too much for your dog which, in its excitement, may take it into its head to run in and see if there are any more that need pushing up, or take off to retrieve a shot bird. In any event, you will be out.

So be ready, with whistle and voice, to make absolutely sure that the dog sits immediately the commotion starts – make sure it listens to you, distracting attention away from what is happening around it – you must be concentrating 100 per cent on your dog, and must be sure that you yourself are not distracted by the spectacle either. This is easier said than done, but this is one of the most tense, yet potentially rewarding moments in a field trial, where the steadiness of your dog is tested to the limit: but if you and the dog get it right, you cannot fail to impress the judges.

Open Woodland

Open woodland, with trees spaced a good distance apart, leaves underfoot and some kind of bushy cover, rhododendron for example, makes excellent ground on which to run an HPR, and most like running on it. The key thing here, as with any run, is to make sure the beat you are given is covered completely. Don't be in a hurry to move forwards, and ensure that the dog does not bore forwards, taking in too much ground while quartering. Any clump of cover, or, say, a fallen tree with its branches and leaves, needs to be investigated, and any good dog will do this automatically; your job is to oversee this work and ensure that if anything is missed, you direct the dog to make the ground good. Remember that pheasant prefer to remain in the area close to the edge of the wood: they are more likely to be found in the area from the edges to about twenty-five to thirty feet in, and are far less likely to be found in the middle, so it is imperative that the edges are covered, right up to the very edge – it happens time and again on a trial that a dog turns fractionally short of the edge of the wood, up goes a pheasant just beyond where it turned, and you are eliminated.

Note that woodcock are likely to be found in wet or damp woodland with bracken, and a point on a woodcock is a good find indeed. Unfortunately for the competitor they make a very difficult target: small and fast with a jinking low flight pattern, it takes a very good shot to hit one of these birds. Some dogs don't like the taste of them and are reluctant to retrieve them, or will not retrieve them at all.

Hedges

Hedgerows are frequently encountered on field trials, as they are on any kind of rough shoot, and working them is straightforward when running into a head wind: let the dog off and let it get on with it. It is rare that the wind is blowing directly down the hedge line, more usually blowing at some angle to it and so through it. The dog will automatically put itself on the lee side of the hedge – that is, the side not facing the wind – and work up the hedge line with the wind carrying the scent to it. This could be a problem if you have positioned yourself on one side of the hedge and the dog has decided the other side is better for it, leaving you without sight of your dog and unable to anything if it happens to go on point. It is therefore better to work out on which side the wind will be coming through the hedge before you start the run, because then you can position yourself correctly from the beginning.

It is perfectly acceptable to discuss your positioning with the judges, who in any case will also have to make a similar decision, as it is usual to have one judge on each side of the hedge along with a Gun. While the judges will be following on behind, each Gun should be briefed to walk just in front of the working dog but out about ten to fifteen yards from the hedge itself. With an eager, fast-working dog they may have their work cut out just keeping up, but you as the handler should determine the rate of progress, and proceed at no more than a reasonable walking pace.

It may be tempting to whistle back a dog that has gone on too far ahead, but be careful not to disturb a dog that could well be intent on heading off a bird running up the middle of the hedge, as they very often do.

Working a hedge on a back wind requires a slightly different technique, because as the dog runs away from you down the hedge line it will have the wind behind it, so it is at an immediate disadvantage in terms of being able to scent game. The trick here is to let it run for 100 yards, say, and then pip it on the whistle to make it run back towards you, when it will now be running into the wind. A bird in the middle of a hedge may well have its scent disrupted by its immediate surroundings, with the result that the dog may not exhibit its normal pointing behaviour, often showing a certain tentativeness, an uncertainty, moving its head or a paw up rather than demonstrating a solid, staunch point with the tail extended with the head motionless. In either case, claim the point with the judges and get the dog to flush when they signal you to.

Flushing in the Hedge
A dog may well move into the middle of the hedge if it can, and will move up behind the game in front, not always the best strategy as this merely serves to push it on faster; but sometimes the game can be held on a point in the middle of the hedge, particularly if it has encountered an obstacle. Commanding the dog to flush may result in it running fast along the middle of the hedge with the bird in front, but this will not be penalized by the judges as chasing game, as long as the dog sits as soon as the bird takes to the air, for example by coming out of the hedge on one side and flying. Remember, the dog's job is to present the bird to the Guns by getting it to fly.

Tramlining, Roding In

Tramlining is when the dog follows a strong foot scent, lowering its head and running fast in a straight line down the field – often down the wheelings or tramlines. This creates a problem for the handler, first because the dog may go a very long way and not be productive – it doesn't find or point any game – and second because the dog must then be brought all the way back to work the ground it hadn't covered before it took off. If it doesn't come back exactly the way it came, and as it is now running downwind, it risks running into and bumping game, which would result in elimination.

Alternatively the dog goes a long way and then goes on point. The problem here is that if the dog does not produce a bird from this point (is non-productive) then you and the Guns and the judges have trailed all the way up to it leaving

Make sure you go back and cover your ground.

a large amount of uncovered ground. If the dog does produce, all well and good; if not, you must go all the way back to where you were, with Guns and judges, before this episode occurred, and cover the ground missed.

You are well within your rights when this happens to ask the gallery and the Guns to stay where they are, and to consult with the judges quickly to agree how many Guns to take up to the dog. Make sure that this mini party stays close together to minimize ground disturbance. As you get nearer to the dog, fan out so as not to push the dog on to the bird. If the point turns out to be unproductive, or if the bird is not shot following a successful flush, then you will have to collect the Guns and judge together and walk back with the dog to the others, being careful to leave uncovered ground as undisturbed as possible. Then continue up the field again in order to cover the missed ground.

MANAGING THE FIRST ROUND

Awareness of the Wind

Awareness of the wind at all times is a good thing for any HPR handler when out on the shooting field, and we have already seen how the HPR reacts to the wind, and the effect on the way it runs. In a field trial it is of paramount importance to read the wind correctly and be aware of how it will affect the dog's run, and the way it will cover the ground. Having assessed this, the handler must then make sure of walking in the right direction commensurate with the type of wind at hand. On the rough shoot, it may not matter if ground is not covered and a bird is missed or 'bumped', but in a field trial you will be eliminated if this happens. Thus in a field trial your awareness of the wind is of the highest importance, much more so than at any other time you are out with the dog.

While all HPR dogs react to the wind, some will make better use of it than others, and while the best game-finding dog is left alone just to get on with it, the less able may need a helping hand from you in ensuring they have covered their ground, or you may need to alter your position relative to the dog so that it runs more advantageously. To get through a field trial everything, absolutely everything, must be going your way, and to make this happen you must be on top of your game and alert to what is going on around you, as well as watching the dog like a hawk.

The novice handler is often surprised by the dog apparently running at a different angle to the one it was following a minute ago, but what has happened is that the direction of the wind has changed, and the dog has automatically adjusted its run to maintain its line across the wind. This means that the handler, who was oblivious to the change, is now walking in the wrong direction. The dog, which usually has an eye on where the handler is, in adjusting its pattern to the new wind direction, has also changed the angle at which it is running in relation to you – and this in turn means that you, not having made any change to your direction, could affect the length of the dog's beat such that it is not now covering ground as effectively as it was. We are now therefore at risk of a bird being missed, and elimination.

The novice handler cannot be expected to grasp all of these ramifications and so mistakes will be made, and you will undoubtedly be eliminated. However, the judges may explain to you what the mistake was, how it came to be, and what you should have been doing to avoid it – and if they don't offer this advice, you can ask them what went wrong.

As we have already seen, the head wind is the easiest for the dog and handler to manage, and in a field trial the judges are required by the 'J' regulations to run dogs into wind, whatever the level of stake, wherever it is possible to do so. In a Novice trial competitors should in theory always be run into a head wind, although the layout of the ground may make this a practical impossibility. Nevertheless the judges will have consulted with the local gamekeeper before the commencement of the trial to ascertain the best way round the trial ground, such that the majority of dogs might expect to experience a head wind.

Nobody likes to run a back wind: the dog is put at an immediate disadvantage, and it is awkward for the handler to manage not only his own movements but those of the Guns as well. Not all dogs can run a back wind well, and it is unlucky indeed for such a dog to be eliminated for a fault while trying to manage a back wind when it is an excellent performer otherwise. The most common problem is that when the dog has run out downwind and starts to work back up towards you (now into the wind), its quartering pattern is not as good this way round as it would be when working a head wind; furthermore the handler now has to work hard with whistle and hand signal to get the dog to cover the ground properly, which is unpleasant and nerve-racking to do.

If you have to run a back wind, cast the dog off and it will start its run straight out in front of you downwind. (Don't worry if the dog disturbs game on the outrun: as long as it acknowledges game so flushed but carries on, it will not be penalized.) The key thing now is not to move forwards until the dog, working back towards you, has covered the ground directly in front of you. The judges and Guns should not move forwards either, and if they do, you are within your rights to ask them to stay where they are. Only when you are satisfied the ground has been covered should you then move forwards, walking briskly to the point where the dog turned on the first downwind cast, as this is then the starting point of ground as yet uncovered.

The major difference to the handler is that the dog is now running its quartering pattern working progressively towards him. This does have the advantage that the dog can easily see any hand signals or upper body movement made to modify its pattern or to cover ground indicated by the handler – but there is a very different

picture if the dog goes on point. The situation might be that the dog is on point, say twenty yards away from you, in front and most likely facing towards you. Normally you would approach the dog from behind, but in this case you will need to move towards the dog along with the Guns and the judges, and in doing so will be walking over ground that has not yet been covered, but which may well hold game that could be disturbed or flushed. However, be aware that neither you nor the dog can be penalized if game were disturbed in this way.

On Point

If your dog is on a staunch point it is usual practice to raise one's hand to indicate the fact to the judges and 'claim the point'. Often the judges can see this for themselves, but there may be situations (for example, if the dog is working in cover) when it is not obvious, and by raising the hand you alert them to the fact that they need to make their way towards you so they are in a position to verify the point, and can assess what comes next.

The handler should approach the dog from the side so that it can become aware of his approach, but is not frightened or 'spooked'. A dog on point can be just on the edge of moving in on the bird, and you don't want to do anything that may cause this to happen – which undoubtedly it will if you approach from directly behind. If you are not sure that your dog will be completely steady on point, blow your whistle very gently as you come closer because this can reinforce its steadiness.

Your goal is to be as close to the dog as possible. Ignore urges from the judges that are designed to make you get your dog to flush while you are still some distance away: 'Let's see it then' or 'Come on, then, get it in the air' are typical, but resist the temptation – this can be difficult, but it is important to get right up to your dog so you are in the best position to deal with whatever happens next.

A German longhaired pointer on point.

Positioning the Guns

It is the responsibility of the handler to arrange the positioning of the Guns, but in practice this is rarely necessary because in the main those who are invited to shoot at a field trial are experienced and know how to position themselves. The more experienced handler may wish to fine-tune their positions, and is at liberty to do so. The pincer arrangement is most frequently employed, with one Gun on either side of the dog on point, away from it by about ten yards and slightly in front. With the dog pointing a bird directly ahead of it, the angle of its nose to the ground gives an indication as to its distance, which may require the position of the Guns to be adjusted forwards or backwards. With a cheek wind or back wind blowing from one side, the dog may end up on point with its nose at right angles to the body, or even pointing slightly backwards, in which case the arrangement of the Guns will be different again because the flight of the bird will be different, as the flush will push the bird out to the right or left (depending upon which way it is pointed) or even backwards.

The Flush

With the dog still on point, and the Guns arranged as required, one of the judges will indicate to the handler that the dog should be sent in to flush the bird into the air. The handler will initiate the flush by telling the dog to 'get in' or by simply clicking the fingers. It will immediately surge forwards, the sudden movement and fast approach leaving the bird with no alternative but to take to the air in order to escape.

A bird will normally try to take off into the wind as the extra airflow will generate more lift to enable it to gain height most quickly (aircraft always take off into the wind for the same reason), and in most cases it will do just that; thus you have a good idea that when the dog goes in and flushes a bird from directly behind, pushing it up into the oncoming wind, it will go up and forwards. Having said that, these are, of course, wild animals, which don't always react as we might expect, and sometimes behave against all logic.

The flush should be positive: that is, the dog moves in immediately on command, moving quickly to force the bird into the air. If a dog goes in too hard, too fast, with the bird just a short distance ahead, there is a risk that it will catch it before it has had time to lift – this is known as 'pegging' the bird. On the other hand, dogs that are 'sticky' on point, which don't move off their point when commanded, or which take a tentative step forwards and stop, then require

repeated urging to finally make the flush, will lose credit with the judges as this constitutes a major fault.

Sometimes the bird will be invisible in the middle of some cover, bramble, thick hedge or suchlike. In this situation the dog will be required to try and make the flush, and must be seen to make real attempts to penetrate the cover in order to do so. Dogs that just dance around the bush or which refuse to try and penetrate the cover may be eliminated. A dog that is seen to do its best, by repeated attempt and by trying different points of entry, but is simply not able to penetrate the cover, will not be penalized, but the judges will take careful note of its efforts and of the type of cover encountered. Credit will be given to the dog that perseveres, and which is finally successful in getting the bird out and into the air.

As soon as the bird lifts, with the character-

A GSP flushes a pheasant.

Steady to fall.

istic sudden explosive whirring of the pheasant, the dog should stop and watch the bird fly away. It is not necessary for the dog actually to sit, although it is preferable, but it should be steady to the flush and any subsequent shot, not moving from where it was when the flush occurred. Any movement of the dog in the direction of the bird and which may indicate unsteadiness, will be severely looked upon by the judge and may result in elimination. A dog that 'runs in' – sets off on a retrieve before being commanded (often wryly called an 'extended flush') – will be eliminated immediately.

The Shot

The bird so flushed and in the air will take its chances with the Guns present, whose job it is to get the bird on the ground, stone dead, for the dog to have the chance of a retrieve. A sporting shot is required: if the bird is shot too quickly – at too close a range – it may suffer significant damage to the carcass, making an unpleasant retrieve for the dog, and rendering the bird useless for the table; but more importantly a bird shot too close will result in a retrieve which is of little or no value in testing the dog, requiring a further bird to be available to it at some later point in the trial so that its retrieving ability, and in particular how soft its mouth is, can be tested to the satisfaction of the judges. In addition, a bird falling in front of the dog's nose, tempting it to unsteadiness, is quite simply unfair to the dog, particularly the Novice. The ideal shot occurs when the bird has gained some height and is about twenty yards or more away.

The Retrieve

Assuming the flushed bird has been successfully brought back to the ground and with the dog steady, one of the judges will ask the handler to

A sporting shot is required.

Judge gives a mark.

'send your dog'. In the case that the dog has seen the bird fall and has had the opportunity to mark the point of fall, the judges will simply expect the handler to command the dog to make the retrieve. If the bird is down but the dog could not be expected to have seen or marked the point of fall – for example, after flushing the bird flew over a hedge to be shot out of sight of the dog – the handler will be asked to recall the dog by the judges, who will then ask you to accompany them to a point from which they require the retrieve to be started.

You will be given a 'mark' by the judge: that is, they will point out to you the area in which they believe the retrieve will be found. Take time to assess the retrieve, whether obstacles are involved, and be certain to check the wind so that you send the dog out on the best line. You will make the best impression on the judges if your dog goes straight out to the mark, picks the bird and comes straight back without any delay. You will not be penalized on a blind retrieve for handling your dog into the area, but it should go out in a straight line in the direction you indicate – it doesn't look good if your dog charges off to right or left and you have to start handling it immediately.

Nevertheless the important thing is to make the retrieve no matter how much handling is required. As long as you do this, you will be asked to continue, with the manner of the retrieve only coming into the judges' deliberations at the end, when they are making up their minds about what awards to give to which dogs. Clearly, a dog that performs the retrieve easily with no fuss or minimal handling will, if other things are equal, be worthy of a higher award.

Take time to set up your dog correctly for the retrieve.

Waiting for the next command.

The delivery of the bird should be to the hand. The main reason for this is that the bird may be a runner, or still alive, so if it is dropped in front of you it may well jump up, run, or fly off, necessitating it to be retrieved again, thereby causing unnecessary delay and distress to the bird, which should have been dispatched promptly. It looks much more polished and competent if the dog brings the bird gently to hand, releasing its grip as you take hold of the bird.

It is worth noting here that it is usual in Novice stakes that game will not be shot while a dog is already out on a retrieve, and the Guns will have been briefed on this by the judges prior to the commencement of the trial. In All-Aged and Open stakes the dog will be expected to ignore any such game taken, and to carry on with the retrieve it has been sent for.

'Eye Wipe'

If a dog fails to make a retrieve after a reasonable amount of time looking for it in the right area, the judges may ask for the handler to 'pick up' the dog, and will then call up the next dog in line to try for the retrieve. If this dog is successful it will have 'wiped the eye' of the previous one, which will now be eliminated from the trial. If, however, this dog also fails, the judges may call up the next dog – and if this is successful it will have eye-wiped the preceding two, which are now both eliminated. Failure here will usually result in the judges going forwards themselves to try and locate the retrieve. If they fail to find it, all the dogs that were tried are reprieved, but if they do find it they will be eliminated.

It is entirely at the judges' discretion as to how many dogs are tried in this manner – usually it is two, but there is nothing to stop the judges potentially calling up every dog on the card to try: I have witnessed five dogs in a Novice stake being sent for a pheasant which was in plain sight not forty yards away in a field but over a deep ditch. Some dogs wouldn't negotiate the ditch, others did but then hunted the bank and didn't get out into the field, another went over the ditch and out into the field, but then ran past the bird on the wrong side (so had no chance of scenting it) and came back again without it. My GSP was dog six and made the retrieve. The judges afterwards said that they would have had no hesitation in going through all the dogs if necessary, as the bird was in plain sight and on the face of it an easy retrieve.

Checking the Bird
The retrieved bird should be immediately passed to the judges, who will check that it is undamaged. If it is found to be undamaged then you will be asked to continue your run, or you may be asked to pick up your dog and return to the gallery if the judges feel that you have done enough or you have come to the end of your allotted time.

Judges do not always make it clear whether you are in or out. If they say, 'Pick up now and we'll see you later' it means you are still in, but sometimes they just say 'Pick up now handler' or 'Thank you very much', and you don't know if you are still in the running, or not. You can ask the judges if you are still in and they will tell you, but it is reasonably safe to assume that if you have not been explicitly eliminated by them, then you are still all right. If they consider the bird to be damaged in some way, they will tell you, and you do have the right to check the bird for yourself, but you do not have the right to challenge their

Nicely to hand.

The retrieve must be passed to the judge.

decision if you happen not to agree. If you are very new to trialling, you probably won't know how to check a bird anyway, so just accept the decision and go with good grace – which is by far the best way even if you are very experienced.

The judges check the bird by feeling for the ribcage and checking its condition carefully. If the ribs are damaged, stove in or broken, this is evidence of a hard mouth or harsh handling by the dog, and is grounds for elimination. Birds can be damaged by other factors, such as being shot too close, and high birds may sustain damage by the force of impact with the ground. Nevertheless an experienced judge will be able to tell damage that can be attributed to the dog, although it can be a very difficult call to make. If there is any doubt in the judge's mind, however, benefit must be given to the dog.

The handler is prohibited by the regulations from handling any game shot during the course of the trial.

The End of the Run

At the end of the run, which should be at least ten minutes in length (longer at the discretion of the judges), the judges will ask the handler to 'Pick up, please', when you should recall your dog and put it on the lead. As soon as these words have been uttered, the judging of the run is at an end. If they don't say anything more to you, then you can assume that you are still in the trial (if you had made any eliminating faults, then you would have been dismissed immediately after the event) and can look forward to a second run; this may appear to be confirmed if they happen to say 'We'll be seeing you again'.

This can be a false assumption, however, as judges may elect to keep their counsel on the run and instead confer together at the end of the first round of runs to discuss whether your dog should go through to the second round or not. This is likely to be the case when your dog has perhaps not committed any obvious or drastic fault, nothing that would cause it to be eliminated, but has not shown sufficient merit in the eyes of the judges. So you can be left without knowing whether you are in or out.

They will then finish recording their mark or grade for the run in the judges' book they have for the purpose. In particular, they will note any point that the dog may have had, and whether the point was productive or not. Any retrieves that have been completed will have been recorded immediately after their completion (or not, as the case may be).

ROUND TWO OF THE TRIAL

Having completed the first round of the trial by running all the dogs, the judges will confer so as to come to an agreement as to which dogs should constitute the second round of runs; they will then inform the steward, who in turn will inform the handlers by calling out the numbers of those dogs that have not been eliminated. These dogs then each have a second run, which gives them the opportunity to achieve any HPR components that they have not yet been able to demonstrate.

On completing the second round of runs, the judges will confer again and decide which of the dogs that have not been eliminated, can be selected to complete the final phase of the trial, the water retrieve, by consulting their judging books to establish and confirm which have completed the HPR sequence. The numbers of

Judges make up their books after a run.

The water retrieve must be completed satisfactorily.

the dogs to be taken to the water are announced by the steward.

THE WATER RETRIEVE

Before a dog can receive a field trial award, it must demonstrate the ability to swim and retrieve from water. The retrieve is usually pigeon, shot the previous day, or it may be game that has been shot during the trial. In a Novice stake, the retrieve is a simple seen throw into the water, accompanied by a shot fired while the retrieve is still in the air. The dog should be steady and make the retrieve on command. The judges are looking for entry into the water without hesitation, swimming directly to the retrieve, with subsequent delivery to hand. At All-Aged and Open stakes it will be a blind retrieve with no shot fired.

There may be circumstances when the water retrieves cannot take place on the day of the trial, and in this case any announcement of awards to be made are provisional, only being confirmed when the dog has completed a water retrieve within a two-week period after the date of the trial, at a suitable venue. It will be ratified in the presence of an 'A' panel judge, who will then sign the water certificate, which confirms the provisional awards. The certificate must be sent to the Kennel Club, which will verify and confirm the awards.

Chapter 5

Pointers and Setters

The task of both the pointer and setter breeds is to find and point, or set, gamebirds. The setter breeds are probably the oldest, and can be traced back to the fourteenth century, being used in the netting of birds; the dog would range out in search of its quarry, hunting in a quartering pattern until its nose sensed the presence nearby of game, which caused it to 'set' – to stop in its tracks and drop to a position almost as if it were about to lie down flat, its body aligned in the direction of the game. Large nets were then positioned well in front of the setting dog, which would move forwards on command towards the birds, causing them to flush into the air and into

Two English setters wait their turn.

A setter 'sets' a grouse in front of it.

the waiting nets. With the advent of the flintlock shotgun the nets were dispensed with.

The English pointer came along much later; originating from the Spanish pointer imported by army officers following the Treaty of Utrecht in 1713, it was crossed with the Italian pointer (although as with most gundog breeds, there is much debate about the origins and breeding influences), and was originally used to point (locate) ground game such as hare, which a greyhound could then chase and capture. The pointer had the hard running stamina enabling it to cover large areas of ground for a long time in search of its quarry, while the greyhound, unable to sustain its run for such a long time, waited with its handler to be unleashed to course the hare. When flushed from its form by the pointer, the greyhound would pursue it at such a speed that it could catch the hare for the hunter – 30mph (50km/h), with short bursts up to 45mph (70km/h), a speed the pointer could not possibly attain, and which the greyhound itself could only maintain for a relatively short period of time, over a distance of about a mile.

Once again, the appearance of the shotgun had a dramatic effect on the use of the pointer, and the subsequent interest in shooting game-birds on the wing gave rise to the need to find the birds in order to shoot them. The pointer was ideal for the purpose, and its subsequent development concentrated on the finding and pointing of feathered game. The greyhound still chased hares, but it had moved to the towns and cities and now pursued the mechanical version around the dog track (introduced in 1926) in front of the paying punters in their equally dogged pursuit of that long-odds win. Back in the field, what the game shooter now needed in addition to the gamefinding dog was a retriever, not a courser, to bring the shot bird back to hand and on to the dinner table.

Today the game quarry for the pointer and setter comprises grouse, pheasant and partridge. On a shooting day the pointers and setters are accompanied by retrieving dogs, but on the grouse moors, prior to the commencement of the season, the dogs are employed in grouse counts. These provide the gamekeeper with essential information as to the success of the breeding season in that particular year, and enable the gamekeeper and landowner to assess how many shooting days can be held, and how many birds might be offered per day.

THE CIRCUIT

Pointer and setter field trials are held throughout the year and follow a well established timetable known as 'the circuit'. The programme starts in Scotland with the Scottish spring circuit, running from the end of March to the beginning of April, followed by the English spring circuit from the middle to the end of April, then the English summer circuit from the middle to the end of July, the Scottish summer circuit from the end of July to the middle of August, and finally the English autumn circuit in September. In all, the circuit accounts for a total of around forty-two field trials, many of which are held over two days to allow two different stakes to be run, a Puppy/Novice stake on the first day with an Open stake on the second, for example; often Breed stakes (trials open to a single breed) will also be featured.

Speed, style and stamina are the hallmarks of a good dog.

ENTRIES

Entries for the trial are sent to the field trial secretary in the normal way on the prescribed form and by the closing date. A ballot will take place in the case of the stake or stakes being oversubscribed, and the field trial secretary will send out a list of those lucky enough to get a run on the day; it will also show the reserve dogs. It is quite usual for handlers to enter many dogs in the same stake, so that upwards of forty-five dogs may run in a single trial. This seemingly unrealistic number is manageable, first because two dogs are run simultaneously in front of the judges, so the number of first runs is rather in the region of twenty-two, and also because dogs can be discarded more promptly, which can, and does, reduce the numbers significantly.

ON THE DAY

Making sure to arrive in good time, competitors report to the chief steward or the field trial secretary, or whoever happens to be running the day, to collect their armband(s) and a copy of the field trial programme which will list all the dogs entered – those with a run and the reserve dogs – as well as detailing the number of dogs that have withdrawn. This done, the chief steward calls everyone together to make the welcoming remarks and to introduce the judges, Guns, the steward of the beat (usually the gamekeeper), and the host, if present.

Turning attention to the programme, the numbers of any dogs that have withdrawn or which have not turned up are called out. At this point, if there are indeed absentees the dogs on the reserve list will be called, and if present will take their place in the trial, assuming the numbers of the absent dogs. Pointers and setters are always run as a brace (two dogs), so the next task for the chief steward is to conduct a draw in order to determine the make-up of the braces. It is very important for each competitor to have

a programme and a means of writing on it – pencil, biro or felt-tip pen – so the withdrawals can be crossed off and the numbers making up the braces can be noted down as they are announced. The field trial programme will have blank spaces for noting the braces, and the draw will now fill them up.

All the numbers of the dogs present and ready to run are put into a proverbial hat, pouch or box, and are drawn out one by one, each number being called out as it is drawn. For example, dog numbers three and eleven are first out of the hat and will make up the first brace. Numbers continue to be drawn and braces made up until all have been partnered; in the case of an odd number of runners there will be a dog left over who cannot be partnered up, and this one is given a bye. How the bye dog (as it is called) gets to run will become clear later on.

Occasionally a competitor may call out 'No!' when a number is drawn. This occurs if a single handler has more than one dog entered and numbers which correspond to his dogs have been pulled out of the hat consecutively. Clearly it is impossible for him to run two dogs at the same time, and so on hearing the 'No' the person conducting the draw will allocate the number just drawn to be the first dog in the next brace to be made up. The next number out of the hat makes up the first incomplete brace, and the one after that the second incomplete brace.

To illustrate this more clearly, below dogs number four and sixteen have been drawn to make up brace e. Drawing brace f, the number six is drawn and announced. Next twenty-seven is drawn out of the hat, but the handler of dog number six realizes that number twenty-seven is also one of his dogs, and shouts out 'No!' as they cannot be run in the same brace.

e. 4 v 16   f. 6 v 27 'No!'

The number twenty-seven dog is therefore moved to the next brace to be drawn, g:

Braces are drawn at the beginning of the trial.

f. 6 v ?   g. 27 v ??

Brace f is now made up by drawing the next number, in this case eighteen:

f. 6 v 18   g. 27 v ??

and brace g is completed by drawing again, in this case eight:

f. 6 v 18   g. 27 v 8

Note that it is up to the handler to notice when a clash such as this occurs, and with multiple dogs entered, you need to be paying close attention to the draw.

With the draw complete, the trial is now ready to start, and all move off to the trial ground.

Where's the Wind?

Pointers and setters run most efficiently, and indeed elegantly, when working directly into the prevailing wind, so the judges, in consultation with the gamekeeper, will do their utmost to ensure that this is the case even if it means trekking the whole field trial party considerable distances downwind. Even then, when a number of braces have been run and the field has moved as far up the ground as is possible, it may be necessary to trek back again more than once to provide subsequent braces with the same opportunity of running into the wind.

JUDGES

There are two judges, and both start off in the middle as the brace are set off on their task. If a dog pulls further out to the left, say, following its game-finding instinct, so the judge on that side must follow so as to assess its work – what the judge cannot see, cannot be judged. It is to be noted that judges waste little time on dogs which do not quarter with purpose – any pottering will not be tolerated.

RUNNING THE BRACE PAIR

As discussed above, dogs are run as a brace pair, meaning they are run simultaneously; the steward will therefore call for the first brace to go forward to the judges, with the lowest numbered dog going with the judge on the left.

The handlers position themselves on either side of the judges, facing towards them and holding on to their dogs. When the judges tell them to cast off their dogs, as a courtesy the handlers check with each other that they are ready before sending the dogs away on their quest, one dog to the left and the other off to the right.

Ideally the brace pair will establish independent quartering patterns which are nevertheless complementary with the dogs crossing in the middle of the pattern, but the one not interfering in the run of the other. The ideal pattern is shown in the diagram.

Handlers should be aware of each other's position as far as terrain allows, and should aim to keep roughly abreast of each other. If one handler forges on ahead too quickly he could unduly interfere with, and disturb, the running pattern of the brace mate unduly. Not only that,

Judges check the numbers of the next brace to run.

Handlers check that the other is ready before loosing their dog.

if his dog is leading the brace, the handler forging ahead too quickly can cause the dog to run further forward (taking a bigger 'bite'), which could have the effect of pushing it prematurely on to game or worse, causing it to run in front of game – effectively missing it, as it hasn't had the chance to wind it. This will cause elimination if the brace mate, running that bit further behind, comes on point on the quarry that your dog would have been able to find.

Of course things don't always go to plan, and dogs do interfere with each other; in particular young dogs running in a Puppy stake often think it's a great game to chase each other around, or one dog sets about its task with purpose but its brace mate is happy to chase it around for fun. This is a phase that many youngsters go through and the judges are usually tolerant of it, up to a point: but if the playful youngster persists in distracting its mate and doesn't settle down to

its job, it may well be called up by the judges. Depending upon how long they have been running, both dogs may be picked up – the errant youngster may play no further part in the trial, while the other, having done nothing wrong, may simply be put 'on standby' to run again at the earliest possible opportunity, or the judges may decide that they have seen enough and will see the dog in a subsequent round.

When running, the judges are looking at all the components of the dog's work: ground treatment, its style and drive, and above all its game-finding ability. Stamina is not something that features as important in a trial: in days gone by dogs would have been expected to run for upwards of twenty minutes and longer, but in a trial it is the game-finding ability that is paramount. Of course the dog must run for long enough for the judges to assess its characteristics, and it can be that it comes on point and

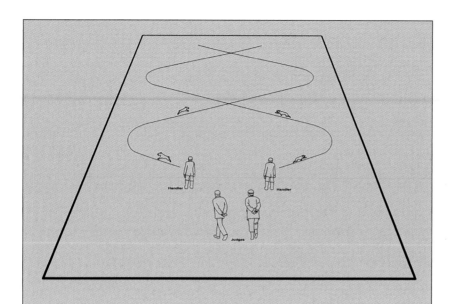

produces to the satisfaction of the judges early into its run. They may decide to run it on in order to make their assessments, or they may decide to pick it up at that point and make their assessment on its next run in the subsequent round. Non-performing dogs – potterers – are quickly discarded: with a large field of dogs to run, there is simply neither the time nor the ground to waste.

Dogs are expected to point any game on their beat, and any that they have obviously missed will constitute an elimination. However, the judges have many factors to consider when considering whether game has been missed by the dog or not. For example on the grouse moors, birds can run around in the heather to the confusion of the dog, and also grouse are notorious for flying in and dropping right in front of the dog, or even behind the line it has been running. Similarly pheasant can run pretty rings around a dog when hidden in amongst broad sugar-beet leaves, and can quite easily run back behind the line of the running dog, completely unseen by the judges, and perhaps then be put to flight by one of the Guns, creating the erroneous impression of having been missed

by the dog. As always, the rule of thumb is to give the benefit of any doubt to the dog.

On Point!

When one of the brace comes on point its handler will raise his hand to 'claim' it, and will go up to one side of the dog: if it is a long distance away, this may take some time, but the dog is expected to remain on point throughout this time, and will normally do so unless it detects that the bird has moved. The judge for this dog will also move as quickly as possible into a position from where the unfolding scene can be assessed – that is, near, but not too near, being careful not to influence or disturb the dog. When the handler is by the side of the dog, the judge will ask for the birds to be produced.

False Pointing
A dog may come up on a point, then apparently change its mind and carry on hunting: it may have been distracted by residual scent – scent left by a now departed bird – or it may have scented something else which has caused it to pause. Whatever the case, these unproductive

On point! Guns ready.

points – unproductive in the sense that no bird was produced – are undesirable, and persistent false pointing is considered a major fault.

The Flush

When a dog comes on point it is expected to remain rock steady until commanded to flush. As we have seen, any forward movement is strictly enforced by the judges and will result in its elimination from the trial. A judge will tell the handler to produce the birds – that is, command the dog to flush whatever is in front of it. The handler, who is by now by the dog's side, will urge it forwards using voice, body movement or clicking the fingers, which will cause it to move forwards until the quarry is produced. As soon as a quarry rises, the dog should be steady, and the Gun will 'honour' the birds going away with a shot, to which the dog

should remain steady – it doesn't have to sit, but there must be no forward movement and no sign of chasing.

The quarry is often one of a covey, and a clutch of several birds are usually present, and in this case it is important to make sure they have all been produced (known as 'making the ground good'). The judge, satisfied that the dog was steady, will therefore ask the handler to work on. Signalling the dog to work on, the dog will either run forwards to check where the birds were sitting, or it may indeed come on point again, indicating that they haven't all gone. The handler will then go through the same process: the dog is told to flush the game, the shot is fired with the dog remaining steady, and finally it makes sure the ground is made good.

Sometimes a dog will not move forwards when asked by the handler, and therefore fails to flush the game. This is known as being 'sticky', and the judges will take a dim view of stickiness: the dog will be marked down substantially in their assessment because this is regarded as a 'major fault'.

There is one circumstance, however, when stickiness may be tolerated: if the dog's nose is pointing directly downwards, it is pointing a bird which is very close to it, and dogs will naturally be reluctant to attempt to flush something so close. This is a good characteristic, because a fast, powerful flush may well result in a pegged bird, which is a highly undesirable outcome, especially as the bird may well be a very young one, a cheeper, trapped down under the heather with no hope of escape. A handler recognizing this situation may signal the judge to come forwards and assess the position. If he agrees that a flush would be counterproductive the lead is put on the dog and it is gently removed from the situation and sufficiently far away to be safely re-cast on its way.

The 'Backing' Dog

When a dog comes on point, its brace mate is expected to 'back' its point – that is, it also comes on point with its body aligned in the direction of its mate, the backing dog 'sight pointing' the dog on point. This is useful in the field for the hunter, as the pointing dog may well be out of sight and the backing dog not only indicates that its mate is on point, but also gives a clue as to where it is by virtue of its body alignment. Some dogs will do this naturally, others may need to be whistled to bring them to a stop – which is acceptable to the judges, but not ideal.

It is important that the handler of the dog on point does not disturb the backing dog unduly. For example, if he moves up right behind it on the way to his dog on point to deal with the flush, he could unsettle it sufficiently to break the spell and cause it to run in on the pointing dog, with disastrous consequences for both dogs in the

Flush! A single grouse lifts away.

Dog on point backed up by its brace mate.

trial. The handler should therefore give the backing dog a wide berth, and be mindful of the need to avoid ground that might not have been covered by either dog.

There are often circumstances where a dog cannot be expected to back its partner, for example if its mate is out of sight. Thus if the right-hand dog has pulled more over to the right, followed by the judge on the right, it could be that due to terrain differences it cannot see that its brace partner is on point, and therefore it cannot be expected to back it. In this situation the judge will instruct the handler to stop or 'down' his dog, and to stand by it until the other dog has completed its flush satisfactorily; it will then be picked up the judge, and the next dog brought up to the line – the bye dog would be a good candidate for this. With the new dog in line, both can be cast off again.

Occasionally the backing dog's enthusiasm gets the better of it, and rather than remaining on point and just watching the brace mate get all the glory, decides it will make a grab for glory itself and launches forwards, past the pointing dog (still diligently on point) and on, to flush the birds ahead. This is known as 'stealing the point', which is fairly obviously not good behaviour and will result in elimination from the trial. Worse, it can happen that the pointing dog is unsettled by the glory-seeking rush of the brace mate to the extent that it, too, decides to run in, resulting in its own elimination.

The sight of a dog backing its brace mate on point is an arresting sight, and one of the classics in the shooting world. A naturally backing dog will of course be held in good estimation by the judges, who will make correspondingly complimentary notes in their books.

The Beat

In the main the judges will want to see the dog's run exhibiting the drive, power and speed which makes these dogs so exciting to watch, particularly on the grouse moors where very few birds may very well be sparsely distributed; little account is taken of the width of beat the dog is running, leaving it to the dog to decide for itself when it is time to turn upwind. Nevertheless, even in this situation there has to be some element of control, because if the dog is so far out that it can hardly be seen, it would be too far away for the handler, judge and Gun to get to it if it came on point within a reasonable time.

A judge may therefore ask the handler to turn the dog if it appears that it is really going out too far, and its response to the whistle will be noted; noisy handling – too much whistling or shouting – is a major fault, which will cause the judges to mark down both handler and dog in their estimation. A dog which is totally unresponsive and therefore out of control constitutes an eliminating fault, which will preclude it from taking any further part in the trial. Some dogs are very responsive to the whistle, while others play deaf, particularly when there is a fair distance between dog and the increasingly agitated handler.

There is also the notion that the dogs should actually run as a brace pair, in touch with each other and covering each other's ground in the classic fashion, and neither indulging in single-minded exhibitionism. But all that said, sufficient ground must be covered in order that game be found, with the apparent game distribution playing a major role in the strategy employed by the handler and the dog itself. With plenty of game in front of the dog, wide beats are just not necessary, but in the situation where game is very sparsely distributed, then the quartering power of the dog truly comes into its own.

A handler reminds the backing dog to keep still.

THE SECOND ROUND

After all the dogs have been run, the judges will confer as to which dogs they would like to see in a second round of runs. In all likelihood the field will have been reduced as a result of dogs eliminated for some transgression or other, and which will not therefore be considered further by the judges. The numbers of the dogs which will make up the second round are passed to the chief steward, who in turn announces them to the competitors.

Braces are made up by ballot in this round, especially if there are several dogs, although this can in fact be done in a variety of ways: by pairing ascending numbers, ad hoc – the chief steward makes them up on the spot – or, more likely, the judges themselves may decide the pairings they want to see, as they will wish to see the dogs they have earmarked to take the top placings run together. If there is an odd number of dogs, one will be the bye dog (as long as it was not the bye dog earlier in the trial – a dog can only have one bye).

The second run is usually sufficient for the judges to be able to place the dogs. This being the case, they will inform the chief steward that the trial has concluded, and all can make their way back to the warmth of the car and the award ceremony.

Chapter 6

Working Tests

Gundog working tests are competitive events usually held outside the shooting season, under Kennel Club regulations; they are very popular and well attended, and almost all the gundog club and societies hold them at some stage in the course of the working test season. Some retriever and spaniel working tests are held in as early as February and March; the HPR season for working tests doesn't really get going until June, and with the shooting season starting in September, some tests will have partridge available as cold game. But whatever breed of gundog you have, there will most likely be a working test for you to compete in almost every weekend.

In the working test there will be competitors who work their dogs in the shooting field during the season alongside a great many others who are happy simply to test their dogs in working

Working tests are very popular with both shooting and non-shooting people alike.

Keep your dog's retrieving up to scratch at working tests.

tests but have no particular interest in, or aspiration to take part in, shooting. For these, the day's competition is an end in itself, and they train their dogs for the working tests alone, many of them performing highly proficiently. For those who do work their dogs in the shooting season and who may also field trial them, these are opportunities to keep their dog 'topped up' and to improve performance, in that deficiencies apparent in a test provide a stimulus to training, with subsequent tests providing further opportunity to assess whether improvements have indeed been made.

For the younger dog, socializing with others is useful, as is learning to perform in an environment where a number of dogs and people are gathered together in one place, providing a wide variety of distractions – he must learn to ignore the surroundings in order to concentrate on the task in hand, an invaluable lesson for any dog.

Many working tests are held in superb grounds that are normally not accessible to the public, and this can really add to the sense of a day out; the Worcester Gundog Society, for example, holds its working test for retrievers, spaniels and HPRs over three consecutive days in the grounds of Sudeley Castle, a stunning location – and this is just one example, but there are many others. Different locations provide a different set of challenges for your dog: if you think about it, you train your dog usually with the same trainer or training group on the same ground, and it is inevitable that even with the most ingenious, inventive training group, there is a limit to the number of different scenarios that can be set for your dog to complete, and in time he gets used to the ground and wise to it all.

The ideal is for your dog to get used to working in unusual settings, where all kinds of

Training dummies are used instead of game.

things can go wrong – and if they can go wrong, they will. This will test your skill as a handler and your partnership with your dog. To successfully achieve a challenging retrieve together is not only tremendously satisfying for you, but strengthens the bond between you, and increases the level of trust – and this mutual trust is the key to a successful partnership and the cornerstone of higher levels of achievement, both at field trials and in the shooting field.

Standard 1lb canvas training dummies are used for retrieving tests instead of game, although working tests scheduled in September may use partridge (as they are back in season); some societies take advantage of this and use them as cold game retrieves, often along with pigeons. While the pigeon is not the ideal retrieve, they are very cheap – partridge will have to be bought in from a local shoot, although

some are lucky enough to have birds donated. If cold game is to be used in a working test, it will be noted on the schedule – if there is no such mention then it is safe to assume that dummies will be used. It is very unlikely that cold game will be encountered in HPR working tests except for the occasional use of pigeon for water retrieves.

FINDING A WORKING TEST

Working tests are staged by gundog clubs and societies, so these are your first port of call: contact the working test secretary or field trial secretary and ask to be sent a schedule. Many societies maintain websites which contain details of working events. For the HPR owner the HPRFTINFO site (www.hprftinfo.co.uk) lists all the working tests and field trials being

Cold game is used at some working tests.

held and is an invaluable central resource. For those interested in retriever and spaniel working tests, the situation is much the same as for field trials, in that if you are a member of a society or societies then you will automatically receive notification of the events they are putting on. Unfortunately this does mean that for non-members it is quite a task to find out about other working tests (as the author can attest) – websites are a good resource, but with the same caveats made earlier. Unlike field trials, working tests are not published in the *Kennel Club Gazette* or on the website.

AM I READY TO ENTER?

Those thinking about entering a working test for the first time are often worried whether they, or their dog, have the necessary skills to take part.

The best way to find out is to go along to a working test as an observer, see the classes in action, and take the opportunity to talk to the competitors, who will generally be delighted to help answer the many questions you probably have. You will find many of the tests encountered described in the sections below: study these to see if you think they could be attempted by you and your dog – and if not, don't worry, as some working tests include a special beginners class, which is designed for those who are contemplating entering a test for the first time, or who are interested in the working abilities of their dog but don't know how to get started.

These classes are taken by experienced trainers who will put you at ease and help you either towards the goal of competing, or in deciding to put more effort into the training of your gundog. The most important thing is to make the first step. If, on the other hand, you think that you are capable of tackling some of the tests, then by all means have a go and enter.

ENTERING A WORKING TEST

The schedule for a working test can be obtained from the working test secretary, the field trial secretary, or simply downloaded from the website; there will also be a standard entry form, which is of exactly the same format as a field trial entry form. This must be completed and returned, with payment, before the published closing date. Unlike field trials, which are limited to a certain number of dogs (twelve or twenty-four for retrievers, sixteen for spaniels and twelve for HPRs), there is no limit to the number of dogs that can compete in a working test, although a society may limit numbers at its own discretion, such limits being published in the schedule.

An individual working test can be composed of a number of stakes: Puppy, for dogs under the age of eighteen months on the day of the test; Novice, for dogs which have not won an award at a field trial or a first at a working test; and Open, which is open to all dogs, but preference may be given to dogs with field trial awards or which have won a Novice stake (the precise definition of stakes can be found in the KC J(G) regulations). These stakes are the only ones recognized by the Kennel Club; many working tests have other categories available but these are 'unclassified', meaning that an award in an unclassified test is not recognized by the KC and cannot be used as a valid qualification for entry into a classified test under KC regulations. Some examples of unclassified classes are:

Special Beginners: For those that have not competed in a working test before.
Special Puppy: For dogs that mature more slowly, aged nine to twenty-four months.
Graduate: A 'stepping stone' between Novice and Open, for more experienced dogs.

Intermediate: For Novice dogs, or younger dogs that have won a Certificate of Merit at a field trial for whom the Open tests would be a struggle.
Veteran: For dogs aged seven years plus.

The first decision to be made is therefore which stake or stakes to enter – it is permissible to enter more than one, and quite usual to do so with a single dog, or to enter different stakes with another dog. A dog under eighteen months can be entered in the Puppy class, and with a young dog this is the one to keep to until you start getting consistently higher placings, when you might consider entering the Novice class as well. Even with higher placings in Puppy there is no obligation to go up into Novice: you can if you wish carry on in Puppy, even winning as many as you like until the eighteen months are up, when you will have to enter Novice. If you win a Novice test you'll no longer be eligible and will have to compete in Open classes. There is an enormous difference in the ability of a six-month-old dog (which is usually the lower age limit to enter) and one of eighteen months, since many of the older dogs, while still eligible for Puppy, are well able to compete in Novice. And many do just that, competing in both in the same working test if they are available.

If your dog is over eighteen months then it can be entered in either a Novice or Open class, but be aware that dogs entered in Open classes will usually have field trial awards or will have already won a Novice test, so unless you feel your dog is at this level, enter it in Novice only.

TEAM EVENTS

Team events consist of a number of teams of three or four dogs and handlers and a non-competing team captain. These events are held both nationally and internationally and are often incorporated into a larger event, such as one of

An international team competing at the World Cup.

the Game Fairs. The CLA has a national team test, but the largest and most prestigious is the Skinners International World Cup; this takes place alongside the Highclere Game Fair, and regularly attracts upwards of twelve international teams which compete for the title over two days of competition. The Kennel Club holds an international team test as part of its prestigious annual working test held at Chatsworth House, where tests are held not only for retrievers but also for spaniels and HPR breeds, again competing over two days.

Individual dogs and handlers are selected by the team captain, the actual method of selection varying from country to country; it may be the personal choice of the captain, or more commonly by a qualification process which goes a long way to ensuring the best dogs are selected to represent their country.

The Retriever Intercounties Working Test Team Event is a national event held annually for teams of three handlers with up to fourteen participating teams. The winning team acts as the host for the succeeding year. Clubs from neighbouring counties often have three-way team matches, and in Scotland the annual inter-club test is always hotly contested.

ON THE DAY

What to Take with You

On the day you plan to attend a working test it is as well to have a 'tick list' to be quite sure you don't forget anything essential – the first and foremost being your dog!

Your list should also include a couple of canvas

dummies, lunch, some spare cash, and water for your dog (and for yourself, if necessary).

The dummies should be clearly marked with your name in a waterproof ink. The 1lb ones are used – don't take the much smaller puppy dummies unless you are entered in a Puppy test and the schedule explicitly states their use. The requirement for handlers to equip themselves with dummies is usually stated on the schedule, but not always, therefore it is always a good idea to have them with you. Those tests that use cold game may or may not also require you to have dummies available, as not all the tests may be carried out on cold game. Again, the schedule will detail the requirement. Note that for the majority of retriever and spaniel tests dummies will be provided by the host society, but it is usual in HPR tests for you to bring your own. This clearly does not apply to those tests which use cold game.

There is usually a break for lunch at around midday, which may last for an hour or so. This is a welcome break for all, especially for the judges, stewards and dummy throwers who will have been working non-stop. Some events do have food available, and if it is, this is advertised on the schedule, but usually you will need to make your own arrangements for a picnic lunch. Some judges, under time pressure due to the nature of the tests or the sheer number of competitors to get through, may take only a short break before resuming. The steward will normally inform the competitors of this when the time comes, so they don't get too settled into long lunch mode. Listen out for the steward calling for your class, which he will do when things are ready to get going again.

You will need money for the raffle. Most societies hold a raffle, tickets for which are sold at lunch time, with the draw taking place at the

On hot days don't forget water for your dog.

end of the day usually just prior to the awards ceremony. The proceeds go to the society, usually with a proportion – or indeed sometimes all – going to charity or to the society's dog rescue scheme.

On a hot day make sure you have water available for your dogs to drink at all times. Do not rely on water being available on the ground – even though there will be a water test, it may be located some way away from the parking area.

While on the subject of hot days, do remember to be extremely careful if you have to leave a dog in the car – always leave windows open, the rear door wide open when at all possible (which should be most of the time, as tests are usually held on private grounds), and consider using reflective blankets over the car, which really do work in keeping the interior cool.

On Arrival

When you arrive, check in at the reception tent where your entry will be confirmed. You will receive a sticker or armband with your number, along with a printed programme which will list the running order for the tests you have entered.

In retriever and spaniel working tests, Puppy and Novice dogs are usually run in the morning, and Open dogs in the afternoon – the schedule will give the details. This can lead to the handler of Novice dogs, having run, leaving the ground and departing for home, and so not being present for the awards presentation at the end of the day. Similarly the handlers of dogs entered in the Open class, knowing full well that they won't be required until the afternoon, may well opt to arrive later rather than at the published start time, thereby missing the opening remarks and notices for the day. While there is no obliga-

The Irish water spaniel is a rare sight at working tests.

tion on a handler to arrive in the morning and stay all day, it is nevertheless expected by the society, and not doing so is viewed as discourteous.

HPR working tests are all run concurrently, and while the Puppy tests are usually completed by lunchtime, the others will normally take up the whole day.

The chief steward will call everyone together to make the initial announcements, he will introduce the judges and the other stewards, point out the location of the various test areas, and give out any other housekeeping notices. This done, it is up to you to find your way to the first test.

The Test Stewards

The steward manages the list of those scheduled to run in the test: he is the liaison between the judge and competitors, the judge relying on the steward to have the next dog ready to run when required. Report to your steward as soon as you arrive, and they will check you off on their list of runners. And once you are there, don't leave without first telling the steward: it is a courtesy and will spare him the hassle of trying to find where you've got to if you are next on to run.

Dogs are run in the numerical order published in the programme, but it is not obligatory to do so, and there are usually departures to the published order for a variety of reasons. It is usual for those who are running in more than

Taking a well earned break.

one test to be given priority, and to run them as soon as possible so they can then go off immediately and complete tests in their other categories. Therefore when reporting to the steward, indicate to them that you are running in another test. At some events, the stewards' list will already indicate those who have multiple entries, but check with them anyway.

It is important to realize that it is not a right to take your run in front of others, but a courtesy afforded to you by the steward and your fellow competitors. It does not go down well if you bounce up and brightly demand that you run next and in front of others who may well have been waiting some considerable time for their turn. Be considerate, tell the steward, if you have not already done so, that you are in another test and then leave it up to them to fit you into the running order.

Each test has a steward, at least one judge, and one or more helpers to throw dummies or fire a dummy launcher or the shotgun. The steward is responsible for the smooth running of the class by making sure the competitors are ready to go forward to start their tests when the judge signals 'Next Dog!', checking that those who arrive are on the list and in the correct test, as well as performing the necessary juggling acts with those who are booked in to more than one.

Tests are set by the working test secretary in consultation with the judges, by the judges themselves, or by the society's working test committee. Ideally, the tests should be such that they are well within the expected ability level. If the tests are too easy, they are really no test, but if, on the other hand, they are too difficult and only a minority of the dogs are able to complete them, then the test fails as a method of enabling a comparison of relative ability. The test is at the right level when every dog is able to complete it, but not too easily!

The judge then has the task of scoring how well the test was completed by each dog, resulting in a much more satisfactory comparison of the working abilities of those on the day,

which is the whole point of the working test. Some working test secretaries do seem to delight in conjuring up the most devilishly difficult tests in order 'to sort them all out', which to my mind is completely the wrong thing to do – the tests are not there to eliminate all but the most capable (or just lucky) dogs, but to reveal the comparative abilities of all the dogs.

'Next Dog!'

This is the universal signal for the next dog to do the test to come up to the judge. Make sure you give your number to the judge so that your mark goes in the right place. Dogs are usually run in numerical order but not always – the judge cannot assume that as number nine has just run, the next dog will be number ten, so do give your number when you are called up or sent forward by the steward.

The judge will explain to each handler the nature of the test in detail, what will happen (for example a shot is fired, then a dummy will be thrown), and what is expected of the handler and the dog in order for them to complete the test satisfactorily. Listen carefully, and do ask if something is not clear. Make sure you are absolutely clear on what the test consists of, and how it is to be done, so do ask again if you are not sure. Most tests require a sequence to be followed, and this must be done to the letter: points will be deducted or a zero score recorded if the required sequence is not followed. Very importantly, always wait for the judge to tell you to 'send your dog' before sending it on its way. The exception is if the judge says 'in your own time' to you.

When you are clear and happy to proceed, remove the lead, *put it in your pocket* out of the way, and send your dog.

Typical Working Tests

Typical tests you will encounter at retriever, spaniel and HPR working tests are described in

Take time to set up your dog correctly.

the following sections. As the organization of each test is down to the society, there are variations in how individual working tests are set and they will differ one from another, so this is by no means an exhaustive list; however, it is a useful guide not only for the beginner who will want to know what to expect, but also for those who are moving up to the next level and have no idea what to expect if they have never competed in a higher one before. It is a very good idea to watch the other tests if you have the opportunity, to see what is required and to see how the tasks are done by the dog and handler, and it is very instructive in any case to watch the top handlers at work.

RETRIEVER WORKING TESTS

A retriever working test usually consists of a simulated walked-up drive, at least two further retrieves and a water retrieve. For the drive, a draw takes place to determine the running order; all the dogs' names go into the draw and are assigned a sequential number (starting from one) as they are drawn out. Numbered armbands are sometimes given to each handler to wear while competing, and numbered stickers are also common – but whatever the method, make sure you remember your number! If a handler has a dog entered in more than one test (for example, in both Novice and Open classes) or more than one dog entered in multiple tests, the secretary may assign non-consecutive numbers in order to avoid wasting time in changing dogs.

The Walked-Up Drive

The walked-up drive simulates what would happen on a real day's shooting or at a field trial, and usually consists of four dogs, with the lowest number to the right of the line. It is the responsibility of the steward to ensure that the correct number of dogs is available to go forward to the line, and to ensure that each handler knows their position in the line. For various reasons – as, for example, competing in another test – the next higher number dog may not be available, so the steward will call the next available dog, in increasing numerical order, to make up the line. Having sent the first line forward to be judged, the steward immediately sets about assembling the next line from the competitors available so that it can be sent forward when required, thereby saving time.

Two judges are normally present, one positioned to the right of the line and one on the left, each judging the two dogs in front of them. Also in line is a game carrier, whose job is to collect the dummies or cold game from the judges when the retrieves have been completed, and the Gun(s). Sometimes a walking Gun is positioned well in front of the line, with a dummy (or cold game) thrower a little further forward.

With the line in place, dogs off the lead and sitting beside the handler, one of the judges will call for the line to move forward. After a short distance, enough for the judges to be able to assess the heel position of the dogs, one of the judges will signal to the Gun, who fires a blank shot. The dummy thrower will throw a dummy or cold game in clear view of the line, usually in front of it but on some tests the mark may well be thrown behind. On hearing the Gun's report, the line halts and the dogs are expected to sit. One of the judges will call out the number of one of the handlers in the line, indicating that his dog should be sent to retrieve the mark.

The thrower will have been briefed beforehand as to where the marks are to be thrown; the

A simulated walk-up.

The judge hands the retrieve to the game carrier.

One judge for two dogs.

four retrieves are usually arranged such that if a mark lands in front of, for example, the dogs on the left-hand side of the line, then one of the two dogs on the right of the line will be sent for it, and vice versa. The thrower must therefore throw two retrieves to land in front of the left-hand side of the line, and two in front of the right.

The retrieve to hand, the handler passes it to the judge, who gives it to the game carrier. The line moves forward once more until again one of the judges signals for a shot and another mark to be thrown. This is repeated until all four dogs have been tested, whereupon the whole line is dismissed to be replaced by the next four dogs waiting to come forward. There are many variations to the basic theme, and the judges will decide on a method between them before the test commences.

Another common variation is the right-hand

judge sends the dog on the right for a seen retrieve, and then the dog on the left for a blind retrieve at the same distance but in a different place. The left-hand judge then does the same thing, and when these retrieves have been completed, the dogs change sides and the line moves forward once more.

This time, when the right-hand judge sends the dog on the right for the seen retrieve, it is the dog that completed the blind retrieve in the previous round, the dog now on the left having done the seen retrieve. In this way, all the dogs get to do the seen and the blind retrieve under the judge. The advantage of this method for the judge is that as the right-hand dog is always being sent for the seen, and the left-hand dog always being sent for the blind, it is much easier to keep track of which dog has done which retrieve.

The judges must assess the heel position of the dogs when they are walking forwards, the promptness of the sit when a shot is fired and the line halts, and, most importantly, steadiness, where any dog running in will record a zero score and cannot feature in the awards even if it performs brilliantly in the other retrieving tests. Very importantly, they will also be assessing that dogs are quiet in line: no whining or squeaking. Open dogs are tested in line in exactly the same fashion, but the length of the retrieves is increased substantially.

Simulated Driven Birds

The simulated drive attempts to mimic birds being driven over Guns as they would be on a driven shoot. Often this is achieved by positioning the line of four dogs a suitable distance from the edge of a wood and on the signal from the judge to 'Start the drive', 'beaters' in the wood make a commotion and dummies are

A simulated drive.

thrown from inside the wood after shots are fired by a Gun or Guns using blank shot. Other dummy throwers may be positioned outside the wood.

In this way the dogs are tested for steadiness amongst the commotion and gunfire, with plenty of dummies whirling through the air so that sufficient retrieves are available to each dog both in front of, and behind the line. This can give the judges a lot of scope as to which dog is sent for which retrieve, but they will, as far as possible, give retrieves of the same value – that is, of a similar distance and difficulty – to all dogs in order to make performance evaluations easier and fairer.

There is much scope for variation, with the possibility to add other distractions and associated retrieves; for instance, the Gun may fire behind the line with a dummy thrown, when the dog and handler will need to turn round to be

sent for the retrieve – which is essentially blind, unless the dog has noted the direction in which the Gun was pointing and has cleverly turned round to mark any fall.

A simulated drive, then, can be constructed to test dogs very thoroughly with ingenuity on the part of those setting the test.

Novice Retrieves

Apart from the simulated drive or walk-up, there are usually two more retrieves to be completed, one of which may be a water retrieve. If there is to be a water retrieve, then the other retrieve may well combine two elements, both of which have to be completed, most commonly a seen and a blind retrieve. For the Novice dog, the distances are not that great, of the order of thirty yards or so, and in the case of the seen and blind combined, this may be

Sending the dog for the blind element of a split retrieve.

configured as a split retrieve: first, a single mark, preceded by a shot, is thrown in plain sight and the dog sent.

However, an unseen retrieve will already have been placed by a helper, most usually at about the same distance as the previous one, but often much less, and in a very different direction. With the seen retrieve nicely to hand and given to the judge, the dog can then be set up immediately for the next one without reference to the judge as to whether the dog can be sent – just get on and send it. It is important to understand that when a retrieving exercise is configured as multiple elements – two, in this case – failure in any one of them means failure of the whole exercise, even if the other element is completed satisfactorily.

A water retrieve will be a seen mark preceded by a shot; approximately forty yards is typical for Novice, but it does, of course, depend upon the water that is available. Often the dog will be sent from a position some way back from the water's edge and the judge will be keen to observe the dog entering the water immediately, and not hunting up and down the bank in an attempt to find the shortest route across.

Open Retrieves

In general, and as might well be expected, the Open dog will be required to perform retrieves at much greater distances and of greater complexity. Having said that, the comparative performance of dogs can be seen even when the distances are not hugely long: with the Open dog the judge will be expecting better execution, a straight outrun, clean unfussy pick-up, little or no handling and superior game-finding.

Many Open retrieves are over obstacles.

The dog will be expected to be responsive to the whistle, and to take direction at a distance and over obstacles, and to operate out of sight of the handler.

The Open dog will often face retrieves of up to 150 yards, with split retrieves where the handler will be told the order in which the retrieves must be made. Obstacles are not only fences and stone walls, but also hidden ditches.

OTHER RETRIEVING TESTS

Apart from the simulated drives, there will usually be further retrieving tests, two being the norm; a water retrieve may be one of them, or it may form a further, separate test. Many of the actual tests encountered are detailed below: it is by no means an exhaustive list, as that would be

an impossible task, but is simply intended to give the reader some idea of what can be expected so that you can get a feel for the kind of tests that you will very likely come across. Many working tests follow the same pattern year after year, with individual retrieving tasks the same, or very similar. Others may change completely or partially, or may be varied slightly to keep the handler alert or to take account of the particular ground that is available to be used.

It should be noted that in retriever tests a shot is almost always fired prior to a dummy being thrown, or to precede a blind retrieve, but this is rarely so in HPR tests: the principal reason for this is that individual tests may be located near to each other, and a shot will (or should!) cause an HPR to sit or stop, thus interfering with its retrieving task – hence the lack of reference to a shot in the descriptions. It does not mean that

Hidden ditches constitute an obstacle to be negotiated.

Memory retrieve.

there are no shots made, far from it – reports from starting pistols or dummy launchers are often used in HPR tests, but only when a test that uses them is located far enough away from others to avoid the problem just described.

Puppy Retrieving Tests

The tests in the Puppy must take into account the ability of a dog at six months (the minimum age), even though dogs up to eighteen months of age can compete in the same class. Quite clearly, a dog of nearly eighteen months will have a much greater ability than the very young dog, and may well already be competing in Novice, but never-

theless the tests must be set so they are within the ability range of the youngest. All the retrieves are seen – the dog is able to see the throw and where the dummy falls – and the four tests comprise hunting, first seen retrieve, second seen retrieve, and water. The following is a selection of tests that you might encounter.

Memory Retrieve
Walk the dog to heel approximately thirty yards (or to a marker). Sit the dog and throw the dummy forwards a short distance. Walk back to the start with the dog at heel. On command from the judge, send the dog for the dummy.

'Go back!'

Go Back

Walk the dog at heel approximately thirty yards to the furthest marker. Sit the dog. Throw the dummy a short distance in front of the dog. Walk back with the dog at heel to the middle marker. Sit and leave the dog. The handler walks back to the start and then sends the dog back for the dummy.

HalfWay Back with Recall

This is a variation of the previous test, the difference being that instead of sending the dog back for the retrieve, you recall the dog (whistle your dog to come to you), and then send it for the retrieve.

This is a good exercise in that the dog is expecting to go and get the retrieve straight-

away, as this is what your training has taught it to do, but here we are exerting that little bit more control. It is a good lesson for the dog to learn: not to anticipate the next command, but to watch and listen for it.

'L' Retrieve

Walk from the start to a stake, turn right (or left), and continue to another stake. You leave the dog sitting at the stake where you turned, and either send it for the retrieve from there, or recall it first and then send it.

Seen Retrieve

Sit your dog at the start with the lead off. Signal to the judge that you are ready. He will in turn signal to the dummy thrower, who will make a noise to attract the dog's attention and then throw the dummy. The judge will tell you to 'send your dog' for the retrieve.

Simple Split

Walk the dog forward to the mark and sit him. Throw one dummy out to the right of the dog, and one out to the left. Walk the dog back to the start. Send him for the first dummy (it doesn't matter which one in this test), and then for the other.

Water

The water retrieve is a dummy thrown a short distance from the edge of the water. The entry for the dog is chosen so that it is shallow and gently sloping to make it as easy for the dog to enter the water as is practical at the site available.

Dogs must be able to retrieve from water.

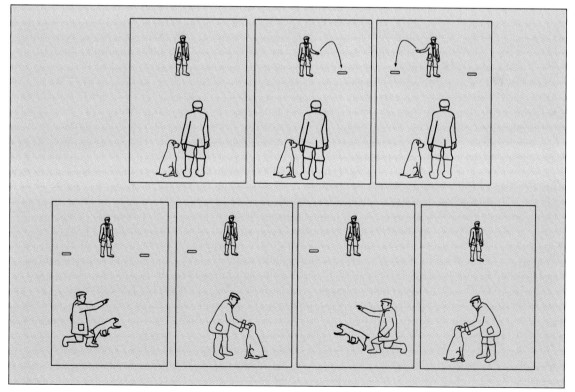

Split retrieve.

Novice Retrieving Tests

In the Novice class, both seen and blind retrieving is expected. A blind retrieve is when the dog has no idea where the dummy is, and in this case the judge will indicate to the handler where the dummy is, or the area in which the dog should look. The Novice dog will be expected to perform quite complex tasks, and should be able to do all the gundog tasks; the handler should also be able to control it from a distance.

Seen Retrieve

A dummy is thrown to land about 100 yards away. There will be some kind of sound made to attract the attention of the dog, a loud whoop or a shot from a starting pistol. The person throwing the dummy may not be in view so it is important that the dog catches sight of the dummy in the air. Often the thrower is hidden behind a hedge or at the edge of woodland. Ask the judge where the dummy will be thrown from (if it's not obvious) and set your dog up to be looking in the right direction before telling the judge you are ready. If the dog doesn't see the flight of the dummy and is unable to mark the point of fall, then the test has all at once become a much harder blind retrieve. Use of the command 'mark' or 'watch' may help to gain the attention of the dog, as it is amazing the number of dogs which just happen to look away at the critical moment when the dummy is in the air!

If a dummy launcher is used for the seen retrieve, the bang it makes will make any dog sit up and pay attention. Sometimes it is very difficult to see the dummy in flight, particularly if the launcher has been angled to get the best distance, and if the dummy is thrown high into the air it may be almost invisible to both dog and handler.

Gun and game thrower wait for the signal at a Novice working test.

Blind Retrieve

As the name suggests, a blind retrieve is when the dog has no sight of the dummy and has no idea where it is. The judge will give the handler a 'mark' – that is, he will point out the area where the dummy is to be found. Note the use of the word 'area': the handler's task is to direct the dog into the general area where the retrieve is to be found, and to keep it in that area (usually by the use of the 'hi lost' command), leaving it to hunt around until it can scent the dummy. Here it is most important for the handler to consider the direction of the wind and to send the dog on a line that will position it downwind of the area of retrieve and so improve its chances of finding it quickly. If the dog arrives upwind of the retrieve it will be much harder work to signal it into a downwind position.

Split Retrieve

The dummy thrower will stand about thirty yards in front and throw one dummy out to the left, and another out to the right, attracting the attention of the dog before each throw by either hand claps or by making a whooping noise. The judge will nominate which dummy is to be retrieved first – and this is the big difference to the puppy split, where it doesn't matter which one is picked first. In this test, marks will be deducted if the dog retrieves the wrong dummy.

Split Retrieve with Dummy Launcher

This test is as the one above, but a dummy launcher is used to hurl a dummy. The bang, the flight, and the bounce and roll of the dummy from the launcher makes a much more tempting retrieve, with the dog all keyed up ready to go. So quite often the test will be to leave the dummy from the launcher and retrieve the second, thrown dummy first.

Seen into a Sheep Pen

The dummy thrower will make a whooping noise to attract the dog's attention, and then

The sheep pen.

throw the dummy into the middle of the pen. Send the dog when the judge tells you – not before. This test is rarely encountered (although a regular feature at one society), but it always catches out many dogs as it is not often practised by handlers; so if you can find a pen or similar enclosure where the dog has to jump in, it would be a good idea.

Open Retrieving Tests

Open dogs are expected to be able to make long, blind retrieves over obstacles (including water) and over distances of 100 yards or even more. The tests are similar in design to the ones encountered in Novice but the distances are much greater, and the blind retrieves much longer and with the dog often out of the handler's sight, and can therefore be very challenging indeed. Most handlers new to the Open class, but who have won a Novice working test, are surprised at the jump in difficulty, and for this reason some working tests have a Graduate or Intermediate test as a stepping stone. As success in retrieving is important in building confidence in the dog, take the opportunity and enter these tests if they are available.

Long Blind

This is a retrieve over a very long distance (over 100 yards), with the dog often out of sight of the handler. The judge will give you a 'mark', and after that you send your dog…and hope.

Long Split, Blind and Seen

A shot is fired and a dummy thrown at about 150 yards. Another blind retrieve is placed at about the same distance, but at some distance away to the side of the seen. To provide extra interest an obstacle such as a wall or a low fence may need to be negotiated on the way.

Blind into Sheep Pen

A single dummy is thrown into a sheep pen about 100 to 150 yards away. This test is not often encountered but is a regular feature at two HPR working tests every year, and always causes problems for many dogs.

Blind Retrieve over Hidden Obstacle

A dummy is placed on the far side of an obstacle such as a low gate or stile (something the dog can be expected to negotiate), out of sight of the dog and handler: for example, the stile is 100 yards down a path in the middle of a wood, and the path has a bend in it.

Double Blind into a Wood

Two dummies are placed in a wood not far from each other, say five or ten feet apart. The difficulty here is that the dog is used to being sent in completely different directions for retrieves, as in the split retrieves, and is rarely sent back out for the next retrieve on exactly the same line as the first: this often causes confusion.

Multiple Blind Retrieves

A number of dummies (generally up to five) are put out at distances which usually vary from twenty-five to forty yards; the sequence of retrieve is not usually important, but all five must be found in order to complete this test successfully. The distances of the retrieves are deliberately kept short in order to keep the time taken to complete the whole test within reasonable limits.

Seen Dummy Launcher with Bolting Rabbit

The dummy launcher is fired and the dog sent for the retrieve. On the way back a bolting rabbit is released across its path as a distraction, the test being that it should be ignored by the dog. The bolting rabbit is a large canvas dummy often covered in fur, attached to a long length of thick elastic: the dummy is pulled against the elastic as far as is physically possible by a helper and held there under tension, then at a signal from the judge, or when the helper is briefed to do so, the dummy is released, causing it to be pulled some distance and at considerable speed by the contracting elastic. The effect is that of a rabbit running across the ground.

Blind Retrieve over Obstacle with Bolting Rabbit
In this scenario, the dog is required to clear an obstacle (a fence or low wall) on its way to a blind retrieve placed some way back from the obstacle. As the dog approaches the obstacle the bolting rabbit is released so that it rushes across the path of the dog just before it is about to jump.

Blind and Dummy Launcher
A dummy is fired from the launcher, with the dog marking the fall. However, the dog must be sent instead for a blind retrieve for which the judge will have already given the handler the mark, the test being that the dog must ignore the dummy from the launcher and search for the blind retrieve first.

Seen Water Retrieve
The dummy thrower is hidden from sight at the other side of a lake: he fires a starting pistol to attract the dog's attention, and quickly follows this with the dummy which he throws up into the air so the dog can see where it lands in the water.

Blind Water Retrieve
A long blind water retrieve is a real challenge, and is usually planned so that it takes place towards the end of the day, after all the other tests, so that everyone can watch. The swim is usually 100 yards or so.

Water Retrieve over Obstacle
Both of the water retrieves above may be so arranged that the dog has to jump an obstacle first. This is not only a good challenge for the dog, but hugely photogenic, particularly on the

Water retrieves are very photogenic.

return when the jumping dog is captured in flight with the dummy in its mouth with water flying off its coat.

Islands

Sometimes the blind or seen retrieve will involve an island, with the retrieve somewhere on the island. A more difficult variant occasionally encountered is when the island is the half way point to the retrieve: this requires the dog to get out of the water and on to the island, which it searches unsuccessfully, then to re-enter the water on the far side, and swim out to the far bank where the retrieve is to be found.

Rivers and Streams

In this test, encountered at one notable venue, the dog is required to cross one stream or small river, and on reaching the far bank is required to cross another to find the retrieve on the furthest bank.

JUDGING RETRIEVES

In assessing a retrieve, the qualities that a judge is looking for in the dog are game-finding ability, good marking, a fast outrun, a clean pick-up and a fast return in a straight line. A dog demonstrating initiative – that is, the ability to think for itself and not relying on the handler for direction – will be credited.

Quiet handling will be credited, as will a dog that exhibits good control when directed. On a seen retrieve, handling should be at an absolute minimum, particularly when the distance is not great, where it could be expected that no handling at all should be necessary. On blind retrieves some handling is to be expected, but the judge will look for the minimum intervention by the handler, and will assess the response of the dog to commands, both verbal and with the whistle.

Delivery to hand is essential, and any dog dropping the retrieve short of the handler will be severely marked down; however allowance will be made by the judge for a dog that stops to adjust its grip.

Common Faults

Poor Distance Assessment of Mark

Frequently seen is the scenario where a dog has obviously been able to mark the fall of a dummy, say at forty yards, but when sent, although it runs out purposefully in a straight line directly to the point of fall and looks like making a good job of it, instead of stopping to pick up the dummy, it runs straight on past it. The handler then has to intervene with the whistle and handle it back to the point of fall for it to make the retrieve.

This is a result of training the dog to retrieve at ever greater distances, so that it comes to believe that all retrieves are to be found at these long distances, and it will believe this even if it is in contradiction to what its eyes told it was the point of fall, at a much shorter distance. Remember that the eyes are of secondary importance to a dog, and that the nose is the primary sensor. Owners are often desperate to demonstrate that their dog is capable of doing unbelievably long retrieves – after all, what is more spectacular for a retriever than disappearing over the horizon and coming back proudly with its find to the amazement of all? What they forget is that the vast majority of retrieves that are made on a shooting day are not very far away at all, say in the region of thirty to seventy yards, and a dog is hardly ever called upon to retrieve from 200 yards or more, as can be witnessed at any retriever field trial. Of course the best dogs will be capable of such a feat, and need to be trained to be able to do it – just don't forget to train for the shorter ones as well.

Too Much Whistle

How much whistle is acceptable is a common issue, and there is much variation in the frequency with which the whistle is used by a handler, and how this usage is assessed by the judges. Some handlers wish to control their dog closely, and use the whistle and hand signals very often to bring the dog accurately to the area of the fall. This propensity may also be true of some judges, who naturally will be more forgiving of the handler who similarly uses the whistle a lot.

Quiet handling, however, is to be encouraged. It is much better if the dog is allowed to get on with its job with the minimum of intervention by the handler: arguably it will gain more independence of thought and be more resourceful in the field if it is confident of being able to locate the fall more or less on its own, rather than looking back to the handler every few seconds for reassurance and direction.

Poor Heel Positioning

When walking up, the judges will continuously assess heel position, to ensure the dog is not forging ahead or even lagging behind. The latter is unusual, as most dogs are only too keen to see what is happening, and are more likely to gradually creep further and further in front of the ideal position. Repeated commands from the handler to correct the dog's position will not go down well with the judge, nor will the dog that persistently moves too far forward. A dog is at real risk of being eliminated in a field trial if it persistently strays too far ahead – as one judge said: 'If its tail is in front of the handler's knee, it's in the danger zone.'

Chapter 7

Spaniel Working Tests

Spaniel working tests often take place in woodland where the spaniel's hunting abilities can be best exhibited. The job of the spaniel is to hunt for and flush any game on its beat, but because the working tests largely take place outside the shooting season and not necessarily on a shooting ground, the chance of live game being found to flush is very small indeed. The emphasis is therefore put squarely upon the hunting,

quartering abilities of the dog, and will account for some 80 per cent of the available marks; the remaining marks out of the 100 are allocated to the retrieving components.

Spaniel hunting tests are organized in a fashion which very closely simulates that of the shooting field, except that dogs are called up and run individually, unlike a trial where two dogs are run at the same time. There will be one or

A handler sets her dog off hunting.

The standard dummy is quite a mouthful for the cocker spaniel.

two judges present, a Gun, a dummy thrower, and a game carrier whose job it is to relieve the judge of the retrieves.

When the 'next dog' is called for by the judge, the steward sends forward the next dog and handler in the order of the programme, who will be greeted by the judge. As usual when called up, check to see if the judge is in conversation with the last handler or in the process of writing some notes; if so, just hang back a little way and wait to be called forward into line. After greeting you, shaking your hand and checking your competitor number, the judge will indicate the beat, the area of ground that is to be covered by the dog, and the direction in which to proceed, and will also point out the position of the Gun(s) and dummy thrower(s).

The usual procedure is for the dog to be hunted forward, with the Gun and dummy thrower positioned on each edge of the beat and ten to fifteen yards in front of the line taken by the quartering dog. At some point during the run the judge will signal to the Gun, who fires a shot, and the dummy thrower, taking his cue from the report, will throw a dummy forward; thus there is a realistic delay between the shot and the subsequent fall of the dummy, to simulate the time it would normally take a bird to hit the deck after being shot.

The dog is expected to stop to shot, and to wait for the next command from its handler. The judge will tell the handler to 'Send your dog', and will expect a fast delivery to hand: it is a seen retrieve, so the dog should be able to go straight to it, collect it, and return swiftly.

There are variations on this basic theme to

Cold game may well be encountered in working tests.

cater for the level of dog, whether Novice or Open, which are described below.

Remember, when you take the lead off the dog to commence a retrieve you *cannot touch it* until the task is complete and the judge has dismissed you. So there should be no pulling it back, shifting it away from or towards you, or putting your hand around its chest to prevent it running in, or any other physical handling.

NOVICE RETRIEVES

For Novice dogs, a seen retrieve is required, and as far as is possible the judge will pick an area of woodland that is equally open for all the dogs. With this retrieve completed, the dog is then hunted on.

Behind, a marker stick is planted in the ground by a helper and another dummy or cold game is placed next to it – as the dog has not seen the fall, this is a blind retrieve. The judge gauges when the distance back to the retrieve is sufficient (about thirty yards or so), and when it is, he asks the handler to recall his dog. When the judge has pointed out the marker next to the retrieve, the handler is free to send the dog for it. This marks the end of the test and the judge will call for the next dog.

Dogs should be steady to shot and the fall of the dummies/cold game, but a little leniency may be given by the judges, especially if the dog has otherwise done well. Quiet handling is always appreciated.

OPEN RETRIEVES

The procedure for hunting an Open dog is the same as described previously, with the dog

A marker stick helps the handler direct the dog to a blind retrieve.

hunting a piece of ground, but this time two shots are fired: in one, the Gun points to the left of the beat as though shooting a game bird out in that direction, and the dummy thrower on the left flank throws a dummy forward; in the other the Gun fires another shot to the right of the beat and the dummy thrower on the right flank launches his dummy into the air. The dog now has two seen retrieves to perform. The judge will indicate to the handler which of the two dummies should be retrieved first, and will tell the handler to 'Send your dog'.

It is very important that the dog goes for the one asked for by the judge: you will score zero if the wrong one is picked. If your dog does set off in the wrong direction, do everything you can to stop it and redirect it. At this level the dummies, when thrown, may not be in full view of the dog (as the case should be with Novice dogs), but the sound of the thump as they hit the ground will be noted by it, and will enable it to go straight to the general area of fall.

With these two retrieves safely in the bag the dog will be hunted on, this time for the blind retrieve, as in the Novice stake – for this once again a stick marker is placed in the ground behind the line, with a dummy or cold game in the near vicinity. The judge will increase the distance to forty or fifty yards before calling up the handler, pointing out the marker as the area of the fall and asking for the blind retrieve to be made.

OTHER RETRIEVES

In addition to the hunting, retrieving exercises described above, it is usual for two more retrieves to be completed. Spaniels are not generally required to execute long retrieves –

Open retrieves may be over an obstacle.

fifty yards or so could be considered to be about the limit of what may be required of them, bearing in mind that their domain is often woodland or ground cover such as bracken, for example, where long retrieves would probably be almost impossible since the dog cannot see very far, and the handler is equally handicapped in his ability to direct it. An exception to this might be when a Gun positioned at the end of the line shoots a long bird on to open ground.

For the Novice dog then, a single or split retrieve both seen by the dog is usual but at a relatively short distance, while for the Open dog it is a split retrieve with both seen and unseen elements, usually into cover or long grass, at a much longer distance. A separate water retrieve

may also be on the programme but is not a requirement.

JUDGE'S RECKONING AND RUN-OFFS

When all dogs have been run, the judge makes a list of the dog numbers, and along with his notes, compiles a total which he enters next to the appropriate number. Simple inspection of the list will reveal the highest scores, and these high scores will be checked to see whether there are any dogs with the same scores and whether a run-off will be necessary to decide the final placings. The judge will know whether places one to three or one to four are to be awarded, and will make up his final score sheet accordingly; in ranking the top dogs, equal scores will necessitate a run-off between those dogs to decide the final placings.

1	45
2	37
3	36
4	24
5	45
6	43
7	38
8	39
9	34
10	40
11	41
12	37

Dogs 1 and 5 have equal scores. A run-off will decide the winner

This dog will be placed third

1	45
2	37
3	36
4	24
5	45
6	43
7	38
8	41
9	43
10	36
11	39
12	35

Dogs 1 and 5 have equal scores. A run-off will decide the winner

Dogs 6 and 9 have equal scores. A run-off will decide third place

In the example above, two dogs will need to be run off, and the judge will give their numbers to the steward, who will call them forward into the line. In the run-off it is usual to hunt the dogs as a pair, the lowest numbered dog placed on the

Cooling water retrieves are popular in the summer months.

The winners pose with their dogs.

right. No game will be shot in the run-off – it is purely down to the hunting performance. The dogs are hunted, and when the judge has seen enough for a decision to be made, they are called up. The judge, having made his decision, can now place the dogs in first and second places. Further run-offs may be required to decide lower placings. Dogs placed lower than the top three or four may be awarded certificates of merit at the discretion of the judges.

Chapter 8

Hunt, Point, Retrieve (HPR) Working Tests

Working tests for HPR breeds are held between March and September and are a great way of training your dog out of the shooting season, as well as a thoroughly enjoyable day out amongst friends. There is no limit to the number of entries in any one class: an average entry would be about ten in Puppy, thirty-five in Novice and twenty in Open; some events attract entries of well over 100 dogs.

Unlike retriever and spaniel working tests, which usually have the classes divided into the morning and afternoon with Novice and Puppy tests normally taking place in the morning and the Open classes after the lunch break, the HPR

Working tests are very popular, attracting large numbers of participants.

working test runs all classes concurrently – so you must expect to be there all day. Puppy classes tend not to go on too long and are often concluded by lunchtime, but Novice and Open classes will take all day to complete.

THE TESTS

There are usually four separate tests which need to be competed: hunting/ quartering, seen retrieve, blind retrieve (though not in Puppy) and water. In most working tests, hunting is marked out of forty, and the remaining three tests are each marked out of twenty to give a maximum of 100 points; however, an equal twenty-five points for each test may also be used.

Hunting – All Classes

The hunting (or quartering) test is designed to assess the dog's ability to quarter the ground in search of game, as it would be expected to do in the shooting field. In all the classes there will be a piece of ground which the dog will be expected to quarter for the judges to assess their performance. The size and quality of the ground varies widely according to the venue, each class usually having its own allotted piece of ground. The length of time a dog may be expected to run depends on the size of the ground available, but assuming this is unlimited, then the judge will assess what might be a reasonable length of time, taking into consideration the number in the class and the prevailing weather conditions. Thus if there are thirty dogs in the class (not unreasonable for Novice) and the judge elects to run each dog for ten minutes, this equates to five hours total time, which will not leave enough time to complete any of the other tests. Furthermore if the day is very hot and sunny it would be unreasonable to run any dog for too long. Adjustments are therefore made on the day to arrive at the most reasonable time.

In Puppy classes the handler may well be expected, at a signal from the judge, to blow his whistle for the dog to stop and sit wherever it happens to be, and then recall the dog again using the whistle, but only when directed by the judge. Another favourite, and one which is becoming more prevalent, is to recall the dog from where it is sitting, and when it is about halfway back to you, to blow the stop whistle again and get it to sit, then to recall it again to come all the way in to you.

Novice and Open dogs can expect distractions, such as a dummy fired from a launcher to test steadiness to shot. The dog will be expected to sit, or at least stop to the shot, and mark the fall of the dummy, which may or may not subsequently be retrieved. Variations on this are that the dog is sent for the retrieve from where it is sitting, or it is recalled to you first and then sent. Alternatively you may be asked to hunt on to the end and send the dog back for the retrieve then.

A favourite in Open is for the handler to throw a dummy out to the left or right at the very start of the test, but the dog is not to retrieve this, but must hunt on up the ground, only being sent back for the retrieve right at the end. In addition, the judge may ask the handler to sit the dog (with the whistle) at any point (but usually towards the end of the run), and then ask for the dog to be sent back for the retrieve from where it is sitting. As it is much easier to send the dog back for a retrieve when you are next to it and able to direct it, ask the judge whether you can go to the dog to send it. You may be refused, but it's worth asking. This has a better chance of being granted if you are the first dog to run, but the judge then has to grant the request to each subsequent dog.

Retrieving Tests

Retrieving plays a big part in the working test, and for many this presents a great training opportunity: you are away from your home ground, so the situation is new to the dog, and

Retrieving plays a big part in working tests.

the design of the retrieve is not in your hands so you will not have any idea of the retrieve you are about to face – and nor does the dog!

At home, on familiar ground, it can be difficult to come up with different retrieve scenarios, and the dog gets to know all the variations and is able to carry them out easily. So it is useful to put it in unfamiliar surroundings and really put its training to the test and see how it performs, and any shortcomings or failures will provide you with a list of things that need to be worked on when you are back at home. When you start out on working tests, this list might seem dauntingly long, especially in the move from Novice to Open, but persevere and value the learning experience. One of my dogs won a field trial award while still eligible for Puppy classes in working tests, which meant having to compete at Open level the following summer:

we spent the whole working test season coming nowhere in the rankings, but learning all the time. But the following season we managed a first in Open, along with a succession of higher placings throughout that and subsequent seasons.

As many of the tests set for the HPR are very similar to those for retrievers, and to avoid unnecessary duplication, the reader is referred to the retriever section where a list and description of the tests that may be encountered can be found (*see* Chapter 6, page 111).

JUDGING THE TESTS

In judging the tests, the judge has the difficult task of assessing how each individual dog has performed the task at hand. The assessment is on the dog, not the handler, but note will be taken of the performance of the team. This is more the case when the handler has to be involved in the success of the task — for example, with a blind retrieve where some handling of the dog may be necessary.

The Hunting Test

In the hunting test the judge is looking for drive, how enthusiastically the dog sets about its task, ground treatment, and control. It should exhibit a good quartering pattern, having regard for the prevailing wind. It should cover its ground thoroughly and be attentive to the handler, reacting to both whistle and other commands promptly. Each breed of dog has its own style of hunting, and the judge will use his knowledge of the

different breeds to assess the dog on its own merits. So the slower trotting Italian Spinone will not be at a disadvantage against the faster German short-haired pointer (GSP) if both do their job well.

With working tests held in the summer months quite often it is very hot on the day, which can affect the performance of the dog — some are more affected by heat than others. The judge will already have adjusted the length of the test to suit the conditions so that a dog will not be expected to run for too long when it is hot. This will inevitably have some impact on the validity of the test to assess hunting ability if the time allotted for the test is short. This is merciful at least to the dog, when the last thing it wants to do on a blazing hot day is to have to go off running in the open sun when what it really

Hunting with drive.

A clean pick-up is required.

wants to do is hide in the shade under the nearest tree.

The Retrieve Test

With all retrieving, the outrun should be with enthusiasm, in a straight line, with the pick-up clean and the retrieve delivered back to hand. The judge will take a dim view of dogs which relieve themselves at any stage of the retrieve, particularly on the way back – although on the outrun there may be a case for leniency, as the dog may well have been standing or sitting for some time on the lead before coming up to do the test.

A clean pick-up is where the dog arrives at the dummy, gathers it into its mouth quickly, and starts its way back immediately. Some dogs scarcely seem to stop, scooping up the retrieve while on the run and turning quickly to come back. The dog that stands over the retrieve looking at it, or which messes about nuzzling it or playing with it, will be marked down. Marks may also be lost if the dummy is dropped and has to be picked up again.

The delivery to hand should be just that: the dog nears the handler, slows down and comes right up, offering the retrieve to the handler who should only have to bend down slightly to remove the dummy, with the dog releasing its grip at the same time. This 'present' does not have to be with the dog sitting down: this may look very nice, and many handlers put a lot of training effort into this final phase, but it is unnecessary as it will not gain you any extra marks – the dog's job is to deliver to hand, whether sitting or not, and as long as it does this

A fast return will impress the judge.

well, either method is perfectly acceptable.

The working tests are designed to show the working abilities of the dog as it would be expected to work in the shooting field, where the handler is only interested in the bird being delivered to hand without any other pretensions. What will lose you marks is a flying rugby tackle on the dog as it thunders past you towards the spectators, or the dog which takes a couple of circuits around you playing to the gallery, or which does a perfect present – but to your behind.

The judge will also note how you set up the dog for the retrieve, particularly in regard to the wind, and although this is not a consideration in marking your approach to the way the retrieve is to be done, it may well decide the outcome

and hence the mark recorded for the whole exercise. For example, if the dog is sent off on a line that will bring it upwind of the retrieve so that it then has to be handled by whistle and hand signal, this would result in a lower mark than the handler who sets the dog up to run on a line that brings it into the vicinity of the retrieve but downwind of it, such that the dog can scent it and bring it back without any input from the handler.

The higher mark given would be because the retrieve was more efficient: marks would have been deducted for whistling and hand signalling, the overall retrieve in this case being less efficient. Marks will not have been deducted because the judge saw that the dog was not being set up correctly and was therefore always going

A sitting presentation nicely rounds off a good retrieve

judge will not therefore deduct marks for a reasonable amount of handling – although the interpretation of 'reasonable' is entirely the province of the judge. Nevertheless a dog that makes a good retrieve with the minimum of handling is clearly going to achieve a higher mark, as would be the case where the dog has been set up carefully with due regard to the direction of the wind, sets off in the direction indicated by the handler and keeps going in a straight line, bringing it eventually to a position where it can scent the retrieve, locate it, and bring it back without the need for any handling at all. The ultimate in blind retrieving is when the dog is out of sight of the handler who, now powerless to intervene, can only wait, perforce trusting the dog to use its instincts and initiative to make the find.

Steadiness
Steadiness to shot or to fall is of utmost importance in the shooting field, and is treated with equal importance in the working test. The dog must remain steady – that is it stops, ideally sits, when it hears a report (at a working test this would be from a dummy launcher or starting pistol) and/or when it sees a dummy in flight and falling. It should mark the point of fall, and *only* set off to retrieve when commanded to do so. In tests requiring steadiness, a zero mark will be recorded if the dog 'runs in' – the judges will give some latitude to Puppy and Novice dogs, and may only deduct a few marks if the dog can be stopped by the handler within a reasonable distance, but Open dogs will be expected to be totally steady.

The Water Retrieve
The key things the judge is looking for in the water retrieve are a clean entry with no hesitation, swimming in a straight line, making a clean pick-up, and a direct return journey. A dog which runs up and down the bank in an effort to find what it thinks is a more suitable entry point will have marks deducted, and is a common fault

to be at a disadvantage, but they may well have something to say to the handler at the conclusion of the test, given as friendly advice.

Seen Retrieves
A seen retrieve should consist of a single command to set the dog off on its way. The dog should then run out quickly, with enthusiasm, in a straight line, picking up the retrieve without any fuss, then returning quickly and delivering to hand. Any deviation from this will result in marks being deducted.

Blind Retrieves
A blind retrieve, by its very nature, will almost always mean some element of handling to steer the dog into the vicinity of the retrieve. The

A Slovakian rough-haired pointer, steady to the fall, waits for the next command.

with many, exhibiting a lack of confidence usually stemming from a lack of practice, or lots of practice but at the same pond, using the same entry.

The entry for the water retrieve will be chosen to accord with the level of ability of the dog: thus the Puppy class will have a very gentle sloping entry, the Novice dogs will be expected to handle a slightly more challenging entry, and the Open dog to go in anywhere and get on with it. A flying, splashing entry may look spectacular but is in fact to be discouraged, as there may be a potentially dangerous object under the surface which could seriously injure the dog if it landed on it. While there will not be any such risk at a working test, one cannot be sure of this out in the field or at an unfamiliar location.

Sometimes the dog may decide to return by land, and in this case marks will not be deducted if the dog, by doing so, did not take more time

than had it returned by water. On smaller ponds, it may be quicker for the dog to run back round the edge rather than swim back. Delivery to hand is required, and points will be deducted if the dummy is put down at the edge while the dog has a good shake, even if it picks it up again immediately and brings it to hand.

Handling

The judge, while not directly judging the handler, will nevertheless take into account the input given over the course of the test at hand. Quiet handling will be appreciated (and not only by the judge but also by all watching), and while marks may not actually be gained by quiet handling, marks may well be deducted for persistent loud handling, whether by voice or whistle – or both. It is a fact that when things are not going to plan many handlers start over-handling their dog, which may not help the dog, and which certainly won't help their marks if the judge decides enough is enough and starts methodically deducting points for each desperate yell.

Duration of the Retrieve Test

At all levels, the judge will allow a certain amount of time for a retrieve to be completed. This time limit is only really required when things are not going to plan, and the judge has to make the call as to when it is really no longer productive for the attempt to be continued; in this case he may ask the handler to 'Pick up please', or he may allow the handler to make a last attempt. The judge may also invite the handler to move forward from his mark closer to the dog and the retrieve in order to ensure that the dog finally succeeds in the retrieve, albeit at the expense of having to record a zero mark.

How long the judge lets a retrieve go on is entirely their decision, but they will take into account whether it is likely the retrieve can be made by persisting. There are all sorts of factors that may come into play here: scenting conditions may be bad, which is causing problems for the dog which is otherwise performing well, or the dog may have just moved up a class and while responding well to the handler, is just not going quite far enough, but with a little coaxing could well succeed. These are just a couple of instances, but all kinds of situation may arise in which the judge has to make the call – often a difficult one. Of course the handler has the right to have a 'good go' at any retrieve, but there does come a point at which a halt has to be called.

THE FINAL RECKONING

At the end of the day, all the marks are collated and added up, which will yield the top performing dogs of the class. First, second and third places are recognized as being worthy of an award. In the event of a tie between one or more dogs, the one with the higher hunting mark takes precedence, but in the event of a tie over all four tests, a further run-off test will be run with the dogs concerned – but this is a very rare event indeed.

After the presentation ceremony all the marks are displayed for each competitor to see; some societies keep the scores on a spreadsheet and are able to print out a score sheet for every participant to take home. Noting your own scores against those of the winning dogs (unless you happen to be the winning dog!) is highly useful: it allows you to identify where and how far you fell short of the top performers – you now know (if you didn't already know) which tests were weak and therefore need more work, and you also know the gap in your performance compared to the top ones – if there is a ten mark difference there is obviously some way to go. As you go through the season you can see how you are progressing, and this is one of the most valuable things about the working test: feedback for you to put into further training.

If you are puzzled about any of the results, the judges will be happy to explain them to you, and in doing so will give you useful tips as to how your own performance could be improved, as well as advice on aspects of your dog and its training needs.

HANDLING TECHNIQUE

In a surprisingly large number of cases the loss of points or failure to complete a test can be traced back to the handler and not necessarily the dog. Of course, the dog is the one out there doing the hard work, but success requires teamwork, and in a team of two, of which the dog is one, the other team member, the handler, has equal responsibility. In all too many cases, this simple arrangement is forgotten or not appreciated in the first place: the dog is set off on this task, is unsure, loses confidence, and comes back having failed, without a word of help or encour-

Presentations to the winning dogs.

agement from the handler who then blames the dog. It is often the lament of gundog trainers that their real task is to train the handler and to a lesser extent the dog!

At any working test you can witness the truth in this. At all levels of dog work, the handler must be actively engaged with the dog to ensure that the task is completed satisfactorily – the dog gains confidence, is flushed with pleasure at the praise it is given, and learns to trust its own instincts as well as the commands from the handler.

When practising at home or with the local gundog group the handler is among friends and under no competitive pressure. Come the working test, the pressure mounts, particularly for the beginner. Lots of people are watching your efforts, and you, of course, want to do well and not look a fool in front of your fellow competitors. If things go well, you quickly over-

come the stage fright and start to enjoy the whole day much more. It's when things start to go wrong that handlers can start to behave irrationally – sometimes they shout louder (because the dog obviously can't hear), or they give a different command (the dog didn't understand the previous command so I'll have to say it differently), neither of which helps the dog one jot, but provides much amusement to the onlooker. We've all done it, and it can be tremendously difficult to restrain oneself from 'helping' the dog.

You need to *relax*, and to judge when to give the dog another command or direction, and when it is best to leave it alone to get on with it. Sent out on a seen retrieve, the only command should be that which sends the dog out for the retrieve. Judges are looking for the minimum of intervention by the handler, and appreciate quiet handling. On a blind retrieve it will be necessary to handle the dog, but it doesn't have to be done with a loud voice, or any voice at all – that's why we have hands and a whistle, and have done all that work in the training field learning how to use them and teaching the dog to understand them.

It is often said that any nervousness, tension or panic in the handler is transmitted 'down the lead' to the dog, which will affect its performance – so try and stay calm. Remember that once you've taken the lead off the dog at the start of a test you are not allowed to touch the dog until the test has been completed.

The Influence of the Wind

The wind has a crucial role for the HPR, relying as it does on scent brought to it borne on the wind. For a dog to retrieve a dummy which it hasn't seen fall it must be able to scent it from a distance for it then to be able to home in and make the retrieve. If you send your dog out on a line that takes it upwind of the dummy, you are immediately putting it at a huge disadvantage as it won't be able to 'wind' the dummy, and you will have to intervene and handle it with whistle and hand signals into the area of the retrieve.

Sending the dog on a line that will result in it arriving in an area downwind of the dummy gives it the best chance of picking up the scent and making a successful retrieve. So always think about the wind. Before every retrieve, take stock of the scene, ascertain the direction of the wind, and plan how you wish the dog to make the retrieve. (The effect of wind is treated in more depth in Chapter 4, HPR Field Trials.)

Voice

The voice plays a bigger part in the success or failure of a retrieve than we would think. In basic training we learn to modulate our voice to impart encouragement with sugary-sweet soft babyish tones, to a harsher tone to impart displeasure and signal to the dog to desist or that it is doing something wrong. The proficient trainer and handler will switch voice tone in an instant to accord with the dog's behaviour. The speed of the switch is key – a dog only relates what it hears from you to its most recent action, or the action it is currently engaged in; thus if it is doing something wrong it needs to be told *immediately* so it can make the association between its action and your displeasure. Leave it even a second too long, and the dog will associate the correction with what it is currently engaged in, which may not be the action you are seeking to correct, which happened some moments ago.

Thus you need to be quick. An experienced handler will have a good idea of what can go wrong, and will have automatic responses which can be uttered immediately. Try to think ahead of the dog, because in doing so you will be in a much better position to correct any error or mistake much faster than if you merely observe the proceedings, are surprised by an error, and then have to think what to do – all lost time.

Encouraging tones are easier to make when speaking softly, but often the dog needs to be commanded, and encouraged, at a distance. What often happens is that we raise the voice in order to be certain that the dog will be able to hear us, but we forget (or don't think) about imparting encouragement, ending up with what sounds (to the dog) like an angry shout. It requires a conscious effort to keep the voice neutral or sweet when we raise it.

Some dogs, particular younger ones, that are faced with too many commands will simply give up. This is also true if the dog feels that it is doing the wrong thing by hearing what it thinks is a voice of displeasure.

Try the following at your training class: walk 150 yards away from the group and have one of them command you as they would a dog. Even if they are shouting at the top of their voice, the chances are you will have difficulty hearing them clearly – and it will be even more difficult if there is a wind against you. Yet back with the dog, we expect that it is hearing us perfectly. True, a dog has better hearing, but the point is really that the level of sound at 100 yards is surprisingly low – which is why we use hand signals.

Hand Signals

Hand signals are extremely effective, and particularly over long distances, distances that your voice could not possibly make. This being the case, it doesn't make much sense to signal with the hand (which the dog can see) *and* with the voice (which it most likely can't hear): the hand signal is enough. When training a dog to understand hand signals we use a combination of voice and hand, but once it can understand and act on the hand signal, there is no need for the voice any more. Quiet handling will be credited by the judges.

Whistle

The whistle should be used at an absolute minimum. It is so tempting to whistle the dog to get its attention to give it another command or hand signal, but over-use of the whistle may distract the dog unnecessarily and may cause it to 'close down' and give up, simply because it feels it can't do anything right, being whistled at every step, and doesn't understand what is required of it. Get to this point and you have failed, because the dog is discouraged and its confidence dented.

Insist on Success

If the test is too much for the dog or things are not going to go the right way, do not allow it to degenerate into failure. It is important that the dog has some measure of success, and it is of the utmost importance that it succeeds in making the retrieve even at the expense of scoring a zero mark. Be prepared to walk forward (remember to ask the judge first) and help your dog make

the retrieve – this is more important than the mark, as there will always be the next working test.

Good Handling

A good handler will be quiet and will leave the dog to get on with its task, only intervening when absolutely necessary. It takes a lot of practice and experience to reach the point when you can be confident in your dog's ability to carry out any one task, and to know when it needs your help, and when you need to keep quiet and leave it alone.

Equally, it is also good handling to correct the dog immediately you see something is not going quite right. For example, if the dog sets off on a different line to that which you indicated the correct action is to stop the dog, bring it back and send it again, this time on the line that you want. It is much less satisfactory to let it continue, either in the hope that it will eventually find its way to the area of the retrieve, or by handling it by means of whistle and hand signal.

THE WORKING TEST ENVIRONMENT

'I can't understand it, he always does this perfectly at home!' This is the horrified observation made by many an exasperated handler to the judge or to fellow competitors whose dog has just completely messed up. The working test environment is very different from the home and the training field, with many more dogs present and a completely different atmosphere, different smells and all sorts of distractions. Your dog will hear encouragement, exasperation, anger and despair being voiced by other owners, and may have to wait quite a long time on the lead before its turn comes around. The waiting can wind up some dogs to such a pitch of frustration/excitement that when it is their turn, they are so euphoric at being off the lead that they completely forget about anything other than having a good run about. Retrieve? What retrieve?

You cannot correct your dog at a working test: mild admonishment is acceptable, but harsh correction is not tolerated and may well result in you being asked to leave the ground. Dogs work this out very quickly for themselves, and this is particularly the case with the younger dog, which is anyway always testing the boundaries with its owner to see what it can get away with – and the working test is the perfect environment for it to push and test the envelope a little further.

Puppies generally are just enthusiastic, and playfully unaware of doing any wrong; they aren't being awkward, but the excitement of the new situation and the many other young dogs in the class just gets too much for them. It is the older, more experienced ones that can play up, realizing that the 'teenage' rebellion goes unchallenged and that they can get away with it. Some appear to play up to it, with the owner becoming increasingly certain that the dog is deliberately behaving in this way just to show him up in front of the crowd. However, it is highly unlikely that the dog is thinking this: it just knows it can get away with it at a working test.

Frankly there is no solution to this, and it generally sorts itself out as the training at home progresses, and as the dog becomes more used to the working test environment, and going to completely new venues is less of an excitement. All dogs, no matter what level, can still be afflicted by unexplained deviations from their normal behaviour or performance, leaving the owner wondering just what is going on. But the vital thing to remember is to remain calm, and to avoid getting caught up in an emotional battle of wills with your dog – which is maybe easier said than done.

COMMON HANDLING FAULTS

At the end of the working test, after the presentation of awards, the judges are asked to pass comment on the performance of their class. Time and again, the same comments on handling are made; the most frequent are described here.

Mixed Commands / Too Many Commands

The panicked handler starts to mix up commands or to invent new ones (clearly the others are not working), so a simple 'Back' command, ignored or misunderstood by the dog, becomes 'Go back, back, go on, go back, back, *no!* Get on back!' and so on.

'Back', 'Go back', 'Go on', 'Get on' as commands may be fine on their own and used in the appropriate context: the first two are employed to get the dog to move in a direction directly away from the handler, while 'Go on' is employed to encourage the dog to keep going – but 'Go on back', although its meaning is obvious to the reader, will simply confuse a dog, which is already confused by the barrage of words, and has probably given up trying to please.

Too Much Whistle

Using too much whistle is the classic situation where a retrieve is going wrong and the handler is trying desperately to control every step the dog makes. Some experienced handlers still have a tendency to do this – even knowing that they do it but really shouldn't. It is much better just to back off, or to use the whistle to sit the dog still where it is for half a minute, which allows the handler to take stock of the situation and work out what needs to be done next.

Loud Handling

You would think that an over-loud voice is self-evident, but some handlers simply don't seem to be aware of their bellowing instructions.

Not Helping the Dog

The opposite fault to over-handling is not stepping in to help the dog when it is looking to you for some guidance. This can be because the handler is trying so hard to be a quiet handler and gain the judges approval that he overdoes it to the extent of not saying anything and having the dog fail. More often it is an inexperienced handler faced with a new situation that they don't know how to solve.

The misuse of the 'Hi lost!' and 'There' commands falls into this category: 'Hi lost!' tells the dog that it is in the vicinity of the retrieve and that it should start hunting around in that area. Note the word 'vicinity': too many handlers send their dog out and immediately start crying 'Hi lost, hi lost!' even though the poor animal is nowhere near the retrieve area. 'There' is used to indicate that the dog is very, very close to the retrieve, being almost upon it. With the handler yelling 'Hi lost, hi lost, there, there, hi lost' the dog is being hindered, not helped.

Chapter 9

Spring and Grouse Pointing for HPR Dogs

Set usually on wheat, barley or rape, the ideal time is when the crop is just high enough to be tempting feeding for the local gamebirds and capable of 'holding' them – that is, the bird feels the crop is high enough to provide it with protection, and so is happy enough to stay feeding in it, rather than moving away from it. This provides the HPR with plenty of game to be located and pointed. As spring pointing takes place out of the shooting season, game can be found and pointed, but not shot, and so the rules emphasize game finding. Cereal and rape fields and the grouse moors generally provide very large expanses of ground which are absolutely perfect for the HPR to show off its quartering abilities, running wide and far in search of its quarry: it is truly spectacular to watch. This is the HPR at its best, and the reason why it is so popular – it is very exciting to watch your young dog gradually get into its stride, its confidence

A Vizsla pointing pheasant in a spring pointing test, watched by the judges.

building, the run 'opening out', running further and further – and then, magically, coming up to a staunch point on a bird.

GROUSE POINTING

As the name suggests, grouse pointing takes place on the grouse moors, and is run in exactly the same manner as spring pointing but with grouse as the single quarry, and with gradings only awarded for successful points on grouse; this means that should your dog happen upon a pheasant, it will not count for the purpose of this test.

For the young novice dog that has never been out on the moors before, this is a demanding test: the heathery moorland is unfamiliar and deep, and high heather can be as difficult for the dog to negotiate as it is for us, so it may take a while for it to get used to the environment. And if the terrain is unfamiliar, so is its inhabitant – the scent of the grouse takes some getting used to, as the dog has to associate the new scent with the bird, and while some dogs may be able to point grouse immediately, some may have a few false starts until they learn the scent of their quarry.

Entering a Test

Events are held by the HPR club and societies, from whom entry forms and schedules can be obtained. There is no formal limit to the number of dogs that can take part, but a practical limit imposed by the available daylight is generally fifteen dogs. If there is to be a ballot due to more entries than available places, preference is usually given to dogs under two years of age; additional preference may also be given to dogs

A young Vizsla points a single grouse.

Participants at a grouse pointing test.

of the breed of the society promoting the event. Suffice it to say, if you have a young dog you can pretty much expect to get a run, while those with older dogs may get the chance of a run, particularly as there are years when, for one reason or another, there just happen to be fewer young dogs about, so it is worth entering.

ORGANIZATION OF THE GROUSE POINTING TEST

Two judges are appointed; one is usually a Kennel Club field trial judge on either the 'A' or 'B' panel, and the other can be another panel judge, or a so-called non-panel or learner judge, as judging a spring or grouse pointing event is one of the first appointments for the aspiring field trial judge. Although Kennel Club judges are normally used, spring and grouse pointing events are not run under Kennel Club rules so its regulations do not cover these events.

There will be a steward whose job is to ensure the smooth running of the day, including making sure that the correct dog is ready to be sent up to the judges. The gamekeeper will be on hand to guide the party round the grounds or moorland, and his intimate local knowledge is absolutely indispensable to the success of the test as he will know the most likely places where game may be found.

The Importance of Wind Direction

After the usual introductions have taken place, the party will move off to the ground; once there, the judges will first assess the direction of the wind. Those gamekeepers who are familiar with HPR work, and who may well host such tests, or grouse counting days, regularly, will

The gamekeeper will indicate the best route for the test.

probably have made this assessment already, and will move the party to a position where a head-wind will be encountered. With young dogs it is particularly important that they are run as directly into wind as can be managed. The game-keeper will therefore point out to the judges the optimum direction for the test, and the first dog will be called up for its run.

Covering the Ground Correctly

Dogs are run singly for not less than ten minutes, and should always be sent directly into wind to foster the best quartering pattern, with each dog getting two runs, one in the morning and then again in the afternoon (unless it has been eliminated). Quartering in search of game, a successful find and a staunch point is a credit with the judges, but the emphasis in judging is

very much on the dog's quartering or hunting ability, and they are watching that it covers the ground correctly and has the correct head carriage for the breed – important for the air-scenting dog.

Correct ground treatment, with the dog methodically working its beat, is most impor-tant. If the dog is covering the ground correctly, ranging the same distance either side of the handler with its nose in the air, then it will not miss ground and is putting itself in the best posi-tion to be able to scent and point any game present. The hunting style of the dog will be noted, whether its head carriage is correct – important for the air-scenting dog – the drive with which it goes about its task, and whether it turns into the wind at the end of its beat. Some dogs, particularly youngsters, may turn down-wind – known as 'back casting' – which is an undesirable feature, untidy and inefficient.

Coming on to point, the handler will be asked by the judge to command the dog to flush the bird: its style will be noted, and most importantly its steadiness – specifically that it sits as soon as the bird lifts. At this time of the year partridge will be pairing up, so it's a good bet that if one partridge gets up or is flushed, its mate will be very close by – so be extra careful in making sure that the immediate area is covered by the dog, especially the edges of the field if they are not too far away, and be mindful of the wind direction to ensure the dog is on the right side of it.

It often happens that the handler, having had a point and flush on a single partridge and having walked forward to handle the dog from the point to the flush (and proud of the good work done, and the thought of a good grading being awarded), then sets the dog off hunting up the field again, but leaving the ground behind uncovered. Then the other partridge takes flight, behind the dog now, and you are eliminated for missed game – and so you have blown the chances of a grading, and the good work up until that moment is thrown away. This is a purely handling fault.

A successful run with a point and flush with the dog steady will result in the judges being able to 'grade' the dog. The judges will tell you immediately at the end of your run if you've been 'graded', though they will not tell you which grade – that will come only at the end. If a grade has been awarded on the first run, the dog may improve on its grade on the second run; but the original grading is not lost if the dog is eliminated on the second run.

Eliminating faults are not hunting, chasing game, not holding a point – running in – and being unsteady to flush.

An Italian Spinone scents its quarry.

A Weimaraner on point.

Ground Requirements

As each dog is run for ten minutes with two runs in the day and with about fifteen dogs to run (if they are not eliminated at some point), it is clear that a huge amount of ground needs to be available on which to hold the event – one dog alone could quite easily cover 20–30 acres on a single run – so large farms with contiguous adjoining fields are used, as well as the vast grouse moors. It is rare indeed, even on field trial venues, to have access to large areas of ground on which to run your dog, so the spring pointing event is one of the few times that it will be able to run far and wide. They are consequently very popular events.

The Final Reckoning

At the end of the day, the judges confer and the gradings they have awarded are announced. The gradings are good, very good and excellent. Younger dogs are graded on pheasant and partridge, while those over two years old can be graded only on the much-harder-to-find partridge. On grouse moors, gradings are awarded only on pointing grouse. Just for fun, an award is often made for the best hare chase of the day in the opinion of the fellow competitors.

Chapter 10

The Working Gundog Certificate

The Working Gundog Certificate (WGC) is designed to provide proof that a handler and dog have reached a level of partnership that enables them to fulfil the tasks demanded of them on a shoot. It is not a competition, rather it is a continuous assessment of work over a day's shooting, although assessments can also be made at dedicated WGC days or at a working test. It is ideal for those who would like to have the work of their dog assessed and recognized as having achieved the required standard for a gundog in the field, but without the need to compete for it. This may suit those who don't wish to put themselves in a competitive environment with the attendant pressures of the competition itself; furthermore for many, the prospect of having to perform in front of a peer group is simply too daunting. For those entered into a working test, the WGC can be achieved even if the dog does not feature in the awards at the end of the day; remember it is the continuous assessment over the day that counts, not its performance as compared to others.

The main criteria to be assessed are as follows.

Control: The handler should be able to demonstrate reasonable control over the dog without excessive or noisy commands.

Obedience: The dog should walk to heel off the lead, and should demonstrate sitting and staying, sitting to shot and remaining steady to distractions such as birds falling, dummies being thrown, and other dogs moving about or out on retrieves. The handler should be able to recall the dog either by voice or whistle.

Temperament: The dog should be able to mix and work with other dogs without undue aggression. Dogs that are found to be gun-shy will be assessed as 'not ready'.

Hunting: Spaniels, HPRs, pointers and setters will be required to demonstrate an ability to hunt according to their breed; thus spaniels should enter cover and hunt through it, whereas the pointing breeds should point their quarry without entering cover, but would be expected to go in so as to flush the game.

Retrieving: Those breeds that are required to retrieve – retrievers, spaniels and HPR dogs – should be able to pick dummies or game in a variety of situations, both blind and seen, over obstacles and from water.

Water: A marked (seen) retrieve from water is required, where the dog enters the water and swims for the retrieve, with a delivery to hand.

Obstacles: The dog must achieve a seen retrieve over an obstacle such as a fence, wall, hedge or stream.

ASSESSMENT FOR THE WGC

On a Shoot Day

Assessment for the WGC can take place on a private shoot or on a shooting day organized specifically for the purpose; dogs and handlers wishing to participate must already be experienced in working with live game gained by working on a shoot. The participating dog(s) and handler(s) will be observed throughout the course of the day as they go about their normal tasks, whether this be on the peg, in the beating line, with a walking Gun, at a rough shoot or wildfowling or any combination that they would normally expect to do on a typical day out in the field.

At a Working Test

Working tests are held under Kennel Club regulations and take place generally outside the shooting season. Retrieving tests are conducted using training dummies or cold game at those tests taking place at the beginning of the shooting season when partridge is available. All the elements to complete the Working Gundog Certificate are therefore in place at a working test, allowing an assessment to be made.

At a Working Gundog Certificate Day

Specific days for WGC assessments can be organized for dogs that retrieve and those that point. For those that retrieve, the day starts with the usual introductions by the steward for the day, then handler and dogs will be asked to walk to a start area, off the lead, so that control, obedience and temperament in the presence of other dogs as well as their behaviour to each other can be assessed.

There are four elements that make up the rest of the day's assessments: a simulated drive, a water retrieve, a retrieve over an obstacle, and a mini drive – standard 1lb dummies, which may be plain or covered with fur or feather, are used for all the exercises.

The simulated drive: The participants are split into two teams, one team acting as the beaters, the other as the picking-up dogs behind the Guns. Each team takes a number of dummies with them, at least enough to provide one retrieve for each dog in the other team. A grass field is enough

Working Gundog Certificates being presented at Crufts. (Photo courtesy Penny Simpson)

for the purpose, but there should be a realistic distance between the beaters and the Guns, of which there should be at least two so that a sufficient number of shots can be fired. The picking-up dogs should form a line behind the Guns, as would be the case on a normal shoot; the handlers will throw their dummies further behind them to provide unseen (blind) retrieves for the beating team at the end of the drive.

At a signal from the steward, the beating team moves forwards, and the handlers throw dummies whenever a shot is fired by one of the Guns; the drive ends when no more dummies are available to be thrown. These dummies serve as marked retrieves for the dogs behind the Guns, and the dogs will be sent in turn on the order of the assessor.

When the marked retrieves have all been collected, the picking-up team moves to one side to allow the dogs in the beating team, in turn, to sweep up the blind retrieves planted by the picking-up team. Once this is accomplished the drive is repeated, but the teams change over, enabling a complete assessment of all the roles to be made.

The water retrieve: This consists of a simple seen retrieve; the distance is not so important as the willingness of the dog to enter, swim and retrieve to hand.

Retrieve over an obstacle: The last element, over an obstacle, is again a seen retrieve. The obstacle should not be too demanding and the dog will not be penalized if it finds an alternative way around, possibly under the obstacle, as the object of the exercise is to assess the motivation to negotiate it in order to make the retrieve.

The assessment must be on live game.

Assessing the Pointing Breeds

For the breeds that point, the assessment must be on live game, so the day must be either a dedicated WGC day or a training day, either while grouse counting or during a spring pointing test on grouse or pheasant. Live game must be present to allow the assessment of hunting, pointing and steadiness to flush and shot; a shot may be fired to honour a flush, but it is not necessary for the game to be actually shot, as steadiness only will be tested. For those handlers wishing to have their dogs assessed for the retrieving elements, which will be the case with the HPR dogs, this may be organized on the day or at a different WGC day or at a working test.

THE ASSESSORS

Those assessing the work at any of the events described are drawn from those who have knowledge and experience in working in the shooting field, and who are therefore very familiar with the roles and tasks that are needed to be carried out on a shoot. They could be field trial judges, those who have judged working tests, the gamekeeper, gundog trainer or the shoot captain or owner. One assessor is sufficient for up to three participants; if more are to be assessed then a second assessor must be appointed, with one of the two being a KC qualified assessor (lists of qualified assessors are available from the Kennel Club on request).

AWARDING THE CERTIFICATE

The presentation of certificates is made at the end of the day, with the usual thanks to the judges, the host and helpers. The certificate will be endorsed with the tasks that have been assessed, as well as whether it has been gained on game or dummies. Dogs that are assessed as 'not ready' in one or more aspects of their work can be reassessed at any time, and the assessor will provide guidance as to what needs to be improved to achieve an acceptable standard.

Appendix A
Kennel Club J Regulations

KENNEL CLUB FIELD TRIAL REGULATIONS
As at 1 January 2010

1. Introduction

a. Field Trials shall be conducted in accordance with the Kennel Club Rules and Regulations.

b. A Field Trial is a meeting for the purpose of holding competitions to assess the work of Gundogs in the field, with dogs working on live unhandled game and where game may be shot.

c. Game that has been handled in any way, either dead or alive, must not be used for testing dogs in any part of a Field Trial, except that dead game may be used in the conduct of a water test.

d. Societies which are registered with the Kennel Club and which have been so authorized may organize Field Trials. A licence and a Game Certificate must be obtained from the Kennel Club for every Trial in accordance with the procedure set out in these Regulations.

e. Notwithstanding the provisions of these Regulations, certain events, which are not licensed by the Kennel Club, may from time to time, be recognized by the General Committee of the Kennel Club. The General Committee shall have power to grant permission for Kennel Club registered dogs to be entered for such events. A Judge, competitor or promoter will not be prejudiced by participation in these special unlicensed events. Any Field Trial not licensed by the Kennel Club is liable to be deemed an unrecognized event.

f. The Field Trial Year ends on 1st February and begins on 2nd February in each year.

g. If, in the opinion of the General Committee, a dog is of savage disposition, it shall be ineligible for entry in any Field Trial, Gundog Working Test or Show Gundog Working Day held under Kennel Club Rules and Regulations. No activity shall be conducted which permits, encourages or develops aggression in a dog.

2. Welfare of Dogs

A competitor whose dog is entered at a Kennel Club licensed event should take all reasonable steps to ensure the needs of their dog(s) are met, and should not knowingly put their dogs' health and welfare at risk by any action, default, omission or otherwise. A breach of this Regulation may be referred to the General Committee for disciplinary action under Kennel Club Rules and Regulations.

3. Stakes

a. A Field Trial meeting may consist of one or more Stakes which are separate competitions at that Trial.

b. Stakes may be run for any of the four sub-groups of Gundogs recognized by the Kennel Club under the Regulations for each sub-group.

c. The four sub-groups are as follows:

(1) Retrievers (including Irish Water Spaniels).

(2) Spaniels other than Irish Water Spaniels.

(3) Pointers and Setters.

(4) Breeds which Hunt, Point and Retrieve.

d.   The following are definitions of certain Stakes:

(1) Open. A Stake in which dogs have the opportunity of gaining a qualification towards the title of Field Trial Champion (K Regulations refer) and towards entry in the Championship or Champion Stake for its breed; in which entry is open to all dogs of a specified breed or breeds except that such Stakes may not be confined to Any Variety Spaniel [except Spaniel (English Springer) and Spaniel (Cocker)]. It may be limited to a prescribed number of runners (J4 refers), in which case these shall be decided by a draw conducted in accordance with Regulation J7.i. so that preference is given to previous performance.

(2) All-Aged. A Stake which is open to all dogs of a specified breed or breeds without restriction as to their age, but which may be restricted by any other conditions which may be determined by the society subject to the approval of the General Committee of the Kennel Club.

(3) Novice. Retrievers, Spaniels and Breeds which Hunt, Point and Retrieve: A Stake which is confined to dogs which have not gained a place which would qualify them for first preference in the draw for Open Stakes. Pointers and Setters: A Stake which is confined to dogs which have not gained a First, Second or Third in Open Stakes or a First or two Seconds in All Aged, Novice or Puppy Stakes prior to the close of entries.

(4) Puppy. A Stake which is confined to dogs under the age of two years at the scheduled date of the Stake.

(5) Other Stakes may, with Kennel Club approval, be promoted by societies, but all Stakes must be clearly defined in the schedule.

Places gained in Stakes confined to Any Variety Spaniel [except Spaniel (English Springer) and Spaniel (Cocker)] will not qualify the dog for the purposes of Regulation J7.i.

4. Numbers of Runners

To qualify for entry in the Kennel Club Stud Book the numbers of runners permitted is as follows:

a.   *Retrievers*

(1) Two-day Open Stakes – maximum 24, minimum 20.

(2) One-day Open Stakes – maximum 12, minimum 10.

(3) Other Stakes per day – maximum 16, minimum 10.

(4) Championship – no maximum number.

b.   *Spaniels*

Open Spaniel Stakes are presently confined to Spaniel (Cocker) and Spaniel (English Springer).

(1) Open Stakes – maximum 18, minimum 14.

(2) Other Stakes – maximum 18, minimum 12.

(3) Cocker and English Springer Championships – no maximum number.

c.   *Pointers and Setters*

(1) Champion Stake – unlimited entries subject to correct qualifications.

(2) Open Stakes – maximum 40, minimum 16.

(3) Novice / All Aged Stakes – maximum 45, minimum 12.

(4) Puppy Stakes – maximum 45, minimum 8.

(5) Where an Open and any other type of Stake are to run on the same day, the maximum number of runners over the whole day is 45.

d.   *Hunt, Point and Retrieve*

(1) Open Stakes – maximum 12, minimum 10.

(2) Other Stakes – maximum 12, minimum 8.

5. Application and Documentation

a.   *Application*

(1) The application for a licence to hold a Field Trial must be made on the official form for the purpose, and must be lodged with the Secretary of the Kennel Club at least 30 days before the proposed date of the Trial. The application must be accompanied by the appropriate fee. Fees for holding Field Trials are decided by the Members of the Kennel Club in General Meeting, and are published from time to time in the Kennel Gazette.

(2) A current Public Liability Insurance Document must be available at the Trial. Failure to have a current Document at the date of the Trial will invalidate the licence.

b.   *Schedule*

(1) A society holding a Field Trial must issue a schedule. The schedule must contain:

(i) A statement that the Field Trial is to be held under Kennel Club Rules and Regulations.

(ii) The definition of each Stake to be held and the maximum number of runners permitted in each Stake.

(iii) The date and place of the Field Trial and, where the time and place of meeting are not included, a statement that the time and place of the meeting will be communicated to competitors separately, and by what means.

(iv) The order in which the Stakes will be run.

(v) Save in exceptional circumstances, the names and ID numbers of the Judges.

(vi) The details of fees for entry and of prizes offered.

(vii) The latest date for receiving applications for entry.

(viii) The date, place and time of the draw and the method of notifying the full result to all entrants.

(ix) A statement that should circumstances so dictate the society, in consultation with the Judges, may alter arrangements as necessary. Such changes and the circumstances surrounding them must be reported to the Kennel Club at the earliest opportunity.

(x) A statement, if applicable, that the society may reserve to itself the right to refuse any entry, except that this shall not apply in terms of the preference in the draw Regulations (ref J7.i.). The Kennel Club must be notified in writing of all such refusals with the society's reason.

(xi) Notice of any restrictions or conditions attached to the Stakes, including arrangements for the substitution of dogs.

(2) No modification may be made to the schedule except by permission of the Kennel Club, followed by advertisement in appropriate journals if time permits before the closing of entries.

(3) The schedule must be accompanied by a separate nomination or official entry form on which the wording of the declaration to be signed in accordance with the specimen issued by the Kennel Club.

(4) The Secretary of the society shall send a copy of the schedule and entry form to the Kennel Club within three days of printing.

c.   *Card*

A society holding a Field Trial must publish a card which must include:

(1) On the front outside cover or title page:

(i) The name of the society and its ID number.

(ii) The breed(s) and type of Stake(s) to be run at the Trial.

(iii) Date(s) of the Trial.

(iv) Names of the Judges and their ID numbers.

(v) Name of the Chief Steward.

(vi) Venue of the Trial.

(2) *Contents*

(i) A statement that the Field Trial is held under Kennel Club Rules and Regulations.

(ii) A definition of each Stake to be run at the Trial.

(iii) The prizes offered.

(iv) Entries listed as follows:

Registered name and number of dog and/or Stud Book number.

Name of owner(s).

Breed of dog.

Address of owner(s), unless requested by the owners(s) to be withheld from publication.

Sex of dog.

Date of birth of dog.

Registered name of sire and dam.

Name of breeder.

Name of handler.

(v) A statement that the society accepts no responsibility for injury, loss or damage to person or property however occasioned.

(vi) Veterinary Support: The name, address and telephone number of the Veterinary Surgeon, Practitioner or Practice supporting the Trial.

(vii) Following the Trial the Secretary shall send to the Kennel Club, within 14 days, a copy of the card with all places and certificate of merits marked, together with the game certificate and a copy of the draw.

d. *Veterinary Support*

Veterinary support compatible with the arrangements for the Trial should be made by the organizing society.

e. *Abandonment or Cancellation*

Any cancellation or abandonment of a Field Trial must be reported in writing to the Kennel Club, stating when and why, and enclosing a copy of the card if available.

6. Judges

a. *Appointment*

(1) The Judges shall be appointed by the society holding the Trial which must satisfy itself that the persons being invited to judge have practical experience of both Field Trials and the shooting field.

(2) Judges may not shoot at a Stake which they are judging.

(3) Judges may not enter a dog for competition at a Trial at which they are judging.

(4) Judging appointments should be confirmed in writing by both the Society and the Judge. When confirming an appointment the Society should include the following wording:

'In accepting this invitation you agree to be bound by Kennel Club Rules and Regulations and the Kennel Club Code of Best Practice for Judges. In doing so you also recognize that you are obliged to notify us in writing of any change in personal circumstances which will affect your ability to fulfil this judging appointment.

You should also note that we reserve the right to cancel the contract before the date of the appointment if there is a change in your circumstances, which in our reasonable opinion would adversely affect your ability to fulfil the appointment.'

(5) All judging contracts are subject to cancellation at the discretion of the Kennel Club in the event of the judge being subject to relevant disciplinary action.

b. *Compulsory Judges for Stakes*

The required number of Judges for Stakes and the number that must be Panel Judges are as follows:

(1) *Retrievers – three or four Judges*

Championship: all A.

Open Stakes: all Panel Judges with at least two A.

Other Stakes: at least two Panel Judges, one of whom must be an A.

(2) *Spaniels – two Judges*

    Championships: all A.

    Open Stakes: both Panel Judges, one of whom must be an A. (If four Judge system used, all Panel Judges, with at least two A Panel.)

    Other Stakes: at least one A. (If four Judge system used, at least two Panel Judges, one of whom must be an A.)

(3) *Pointers and Setters – two Judges*

    Champion Stake: both A.

    Other Stakes: at least one A.

(4) *Hunt, Point and Retrieve Breeds - two Judges*

    Open Stakes: both Panel Judges, one of whom must be an A.

    Other Stakes: at least one A.

c.   *Qualifications for Panels*

(1) The General Committee shall issue to Field Trial societies the official lists of Panel Judges for Retrievers, Spaniels, Pointers and Setters and Breeds which Hunt, Point and Retrieve which will be subject to adoption annually by the General Committee.

(2) Before a Judge can be considered for addition to any panel he must be recommended by a Field Trial society which is approved to hold Open Stakes for the appropriate sub-group and for which he has judged within the previous three years. Before considering the addition of any candidate to a panel the Field Trials Sub-Committee will seek reports from all 'A' Panel judges with whom the candidate has judged during the last five calendar years and in the case of a candidate for the 'B' Panel for Retrievers or Spaniels, from 1 January 2010 onwards, all 'B' Panel judges with whom the candidate has judged on or after that date and for a period not exceeding the last five calendar years.

(3) Judging experience must include Stakes judged at Trials held by at least two different societies. Before being added to the Panel for Retrievers or Spaniels candidates for the B Panel must have handled a dog to win at least one Field Trial Stake for the appropriate sub-group and have considerable Field Trial experience. Before being added to the A Panel, candidates must have handled a dog to win at least one Open Stake for the appropriate sub-group and, since being added to the B Panel, have substantially increased their Field Trial experience.

(4) Prospective Judges for Pointers and Setters should have some experience in judging both partridge/pheasant and grouse Trials before being added to any panel.

(5) Before a Judge can be added to a Panel he must have judged:

    (i) Panel: Retrievers and Spaniels – over a minimum period of three calendar years, and a maximum period of five calendar years, to have judged a minimum of six Stakes with at least five different A Panel Judges.

    Pointers and Setters – a minimum of four Trials.

    HPRs – a minimum of four Stakes with at least four different Judges.

    (ii) A Panel: Retrievers and Spaniels – over a minimum period of three calendar years, and a maximum period of five calendar years, to have judged commencing from the date of the appointment to the B Panel, a minimum of six Stakes of which at least three must have been Open Stakes with at least five different A Panel Judges. Reports must be available from at least five different A Panel Co-Judges.

    For Pointers and Setters – a minimum of four Trials of which at least two must have been Open Trials.

    Reports must be available from at least four different A Panel Co- Judges.

    HPRs – a minimum of six Stakes of which at least one must have been Open. Reports must be available from at least four different A Panel Co-Judges.

    (iii) Re-Applications: Retrievers and Spaniels – a further four Stakes with at least four different A Panel Judges. Note: For the A Panel at least two Stakes must have been Open.

    Pointers and Setters – a minimum of four Trials.

HPRs – For the A Panel a further four Stakes of which at least one must have been Open.

Except in exceptional circumstances for re-applications, reports must be available from all Co-Judges.

(6) Before a judge can be added to a Panel he must have attended a Kennel Club Judges' Training Programme seminar on Kennel Club J Regulations for the appropriate sub-group and have passed the examination.

7. Entries

A dog must, at the time of entry for a Trial be registered as required by Kennel Club Rules and Regulations in the owner's name (or registration of transfer applied for). In the case of joint registered owners the full name of every registered owner must be given. Where an owner makes an entry on behalf of another joint registered owner(s) or where an agent enters on behalf of a single or joint registered owner(s), such person must have the authority and consent from the single or joint registered owner(s) to sign the entry form on their behalf thereby binding them all to Kennel Club Rules and Regulations. In the event of any dispute, evidence of such authority and consent will be required. A dog acquired subsequent to entry having been made at a Trial may compete as the new owner's property provided that an application for the transfer has been forwarded to the Kennel Club before the Trial, and the new owner has undertaken to abide by the Regulations and conditions of the original entry form (and in accordance with the conditions set out above).

a. An entry is an application, on a copy of an official Kennel Club entry form supplied by a registered society, for a named dog, registered at the Kennel Club in the name of the owner, to run in a Stake, subject to any conditions laid down in these Regulations and must comply with Regulation B20 in the Kennel Club Year Book (Regulations for Classification and Registration).

b. A nomination is a request by a named person to enter a dog. In the event of a ballot, those drawn for places will be sent an Entry Form for a named dog, which is eligible for the Stake and registered at the Kennel Club, in their name.

c. A society may make its own arrangements as regards dates of closing of entries or nominations and, except where otherwise defined in the Regulations, conditions of Stakes.

d. A society may reserve to itself the right to refuse any entry or nomination, except that this shall not apply in terms of the preference in the draw regulations (ref. J7.i).

e. If entries or nominations exceed the number of permitted runners, the right to compete in a Trial shall be decided by ballot (subject to Regulation J7.I, which relates to preference in the draw for Open Stakes). The society must publish the result of this ballot in full to all applicants.

f. After an applicant has been successful in the draw for places in a Stake, or as a reserve has accepted an offer of a run, the applicant, if the entry has not been taken up, may be liable for the full entry fee, except where a competitor has qualified out of Novice Stakes or qualified for a Championship after the entries have closed, or on production of a veterinary certificate.

g. Societies must ensure that all eligible owners are given the opportunity of having their preferred dog entered into the first ballot providing it is appropriately qualified. They may, or may not, after such an entry has been accepted, allow an applicant to substitute a dog before a Trial with another dog owned by him: the dog must, however, be eligible and, where a preferential draw is held, it must have the necessary qualifications. Societies, if allowing substitution, must show this clearly on the schedule. Societies may have discretion to confine the handling of dogs to one dog per owner. (See also J9.b.(6))

h. A member of a society which runs two Open Retriever Stakes in a season, and who enters and is successful in the draw for each of those Stakes, may be asked by the society which of the Stakes he/she wishes to run in. This must be clearly stated on both schedules.

i. *Preference in the draw for Open Stakes*

(1) *Retrievers*
A First, Second, Third or Fourth in a 24-Dog Open Stake. First, Second or Third in a 12-Dog Open Stake. First in All-Aged or Novice Stakes.

(2) *Spaniels*

A First, Second or Third in an Open Stake or a First in an All-Aged or Novice Stake. To qualify for preference in the draw in an Open Spaniel Stake, the dog must have gained the appropriate places in a Stake open to its breed.

(3) *Pointers and Setters*

A First, Second or Third in an Open Stake.

A First or two Seconds in All-Aged, Novice or Puppy Stakes.

(4) *Breeds which Hunt, Point and Retrieve*

A First, Second or Third in an Open Stake.

A First or Second in an All-Aged Stake or First in a Novice Stake.

j. In Open Stakes, a society may give preference in the draw to its own members, but this must be given in the following order only:

(i) Members' dogs which have gained places as shown above.

(ii) Non-members' dogs which have gained places as shown above.

(iii) Members' dogs which have gained other places.

(iv) Non-members' dogs which have gained other places.

(v) Other dogs.

The foregoing places must have been gained in a Stake qualifying for entry in the Kennel Club Stud Book. If a competitor enters more than one similarly qualified dog, his first 'preferred dog' must be balloted for in the normal manner. 'Second' and subsequent dogs must then be placed in separate ballots before entries are drawn from other categories.

k. The Secretary of the society shall retain all entry forms of competitors for twelve months after the meeting, and produce any of them to the Secretary of the Kennel Club if so requested.

8. Awards and Prizes

a. An award is any placing in a Stake decided by the Judges which may be First, Second, Third or Fourth.

b. The following may also be conferred at the discretion of the Judges: at a Championship Diplomas of Merit, and in other Stakes, Certificates of Merit.

c. A prize is a reward for merit in competition.

d. All prize money must be paid within one month of the date of the Field Trial, and paid subject to return in the event of a subsequent disqualification.

e. The amount of prize money offered by a society may be varied to relate to the number of entries received and may be reduced if the full number of entries is not received.

f. Awards at a Field Trial must be discrete; equal awards are prohibited.

g. The Judges are empowered and instructed to withhold any prize or Award if, in their opinion, the dogs competing do not show sufficient merit.

9. Control of Dogs and Competitors under Trial

a. *Management*

The management of a Field Trial shall be the responsibility of the society to which the licence is issued.

(1) A Chief Steward, who should be present throughout the Trial, must be appointed by the committee of the Society and shall be responsible for ensuring the regulations are observed. The Chief Steward must not interfere with the Judges' decisions which are final but should, however, decide upon any matter not related to judging which is not provided for in the rules and regulations. The Chief Steward may call upon the Judges to assist with such a decision, and that decision shall be final.

(2) Societies must ensure that the draw for the initial order of running shall take place as stated in the schedule, and each dog entered must be given a number that accords with its place in the draw.

(3) A handler and dog must always be available to pick up wounded game when required as agreed between host and society.

b. *Handling and Competing*

(1) All competitors must be present when the Chief Steward announces that the Trial has commenced, and subsequently when required by the Judges. However, a competitor who is not present when the Chief Steward announces that the Trial has commenced, and whose number has been allocated to the next available reserve, forfeits his run in the Trial. Should a competitor be delayed by circumstances which are exceptional in the opinion of the Chief Steward of the organizing society, then the competitor may still be allowed to take the run, in order of draw, providing he/she is available when required in line by the Judges.

(2) No person attending a Trial may allow a bitch in season to be on the Field Trial ground or to foul any ground to be used by competing dogs.

(3) If, after consultation with the Judges, the Chief Steward considers a dog unfit to compete, by reason of contagious disease or physical condition, such a dog shall be required to be removed immediately from the ground and from the Trial.

(4) Any person in charge of a dog at a Field Trial must at all times ensure that the dog is kept under proper control whilst at the meet, or venue of the Trial, and while travelling to or from the meet or venue in any transport provided for that purpose.

(5) All handlers must carry out the instructions of the Judges who are empowered to turn out of the Stake any dog whose handler does not obey them, or whose handler wilfully interferes with another competitor or dog.

(6) Except in the Championships, no handler may handle more than two dogs in a Stake for Retrievers, Spaniels or Breeds which Hunt, Point and Retrieve, or more than five dogs in any Stake for Pointers and Setters. (*See also* J7.g.)

(7) An owner, having deputed the handling of a dog to another, may be in the line while the dog is working, but must take no part in working the dog.

(8) There shall be no substitution of handler once a Stake at a Field Trial has commenced.

(9) A handler must ensure that only the number of the dog being handled at the time is displayed.

(10) No person shall carry out punitive correction or harsh handling at a Field Trial.

(11) Only in cases of physical disability, and with the permission of the Judges, may a handler carry a stick whilst working his dog.

(12) No competitor may withdraw a dog or leave the Trial ground without the permission of a Judge or Chief Steward.

(13) There is an established code of conduct expected at Field Trials and those taking part in them shall not openly impugn the decision of the Judge or Judges or criticize the host, ground or Guns.

10. Championships and Champion Stake

a. The following Championships and Champion Stake may be held annually:

(1) The IGL Retriever Championship.

(2) The English Springer Spaniel Championship.

(3) The Cocker Spaniel Championship.

(4) The Pointer and Setter Champion Stake.

(5) The Hunt, Point and Retrieve Championship.

b. The conditions governing the Championships and Champion Stake and the lists of societies approved to hold Open Stakes shall be reviewed annually by the General Committee and published as early as possible each year in the Kennel Gazette.

11. Removal of Dog(s) From the Trial

A dog shall be removed from the Trial if it is:

a.   A bitch which is in season.

b.   Suffering from any infectious or contagious disease.

c.   Interfering with the safety or chance of winning of an opponent.

d.   Of such temperament or is so much out of control as to be a danger to the safety of any person or other animal.

e.   Likely to cause suffering to the dog if it continues competing.

12. Objections

a.   An objection to a breach of Kennel Club Regulation(s) may be made direct to the Secretary of the Trial before the end of the Trial. As an alternative, an objection may be lodged directly with the Kennel Club within seven days after the last day of the Trial, and under these circumstances a copy of the objection must be sent to the Field Trial Secretary. When an objection is lodged the following information must be given:

    A statement detailing the objection, quoting the relevant Regulation(s).

    The objection fee of £35, or such amount as may from time to time be decided by the General Committee.

    The name and address of the objector.

    The name and address of the owner of the dog (if relevant).

    All relevant evidence.

    The objection fee may be returned after consideration of the objection.

b.   The right to lodge an objection to a dog or any action taken at a Trial is limited to anyone in attendance at the Trial, or the owner of a dog competing or his accredited representative, provided they are not under a term of suspension imposed by the Kennel Club.

c.   No objection shall be invalidated solely on the grounds that it was incorrectly lodged.

d.   With the exception of objections made under J11, the dog should be allowed to compete and a full report made to the Kennel Club.

e.   Objections or alleged breaches of Kennel Club Regulations shall be referred to the General Committee of the Kennel Club who have the power to delegate the hearing of the objection or breach of Regulation to the relevant sub-committee or may decide to refer the matter for disciplinary action under Kennel Club Rule A42.

f.   Any appeal against the relevant sub-committee decision must be lodged within fourteen days of the decision being given and will be subject to the prescribed appeals procedure as shall be determined by the General Committee from time to time.

13. Disqualification and Forfeit of Awards

a.   A dog may be disqualified by the General Committee from winning an award, whether an objection has been lodged or not, if it is proved amongst other things:

    (1) To have undergone surgical interference with the structure of the vocal cords for non-therapeutic reasons.

    (2) To have been entered for a Field Trial not recognized by the General Committee.

    (3) To have been entered by a person disqualified or suspended under Kennel Club Rules.

    (4) To have been entered for a Field Trial not in accordance with the Regulations of the Kennel Club.

    (5) To have been registered or recorded as owned by one of the scheduled Judges within a period of twelve months prior to the Trial. This provision does not apply to Judges appointed in an emergency.

    (6) To have been handled at a Trial, boarded or prepared for competition by one of the scheduled Judges within the previous twelve months prior to the Trial. This provision does not apply to Judges appointed in an emergency.

    (7) To have been the subject of any other default, omission, action or incident occurring at or in connection with the Trial rendering it unfair that the award should be allowed to stand.

(8) If a dog be disqualified, the prize to which it would otherwise have been entitled shall be forfeited. The Committee may at its discretion move up the dog or dogs next in order of merit (up to and including reserve or fourth place) to take the prize or prize(s).

14. Fraudulent or Discreditable Conduct at Trials

a.   The organizing society of a Trial must immediately report in writing to the Secretary of the Kennel Club any case of alleged fraudulent or discreditable conduct, or any default, omission or incident at, or in connection with, the Trial which may come to its notice, even where parties concerned have indicated that they intend taking no action. The society, at the same time, must forward to the Secretary of the Kennel Club all documents and information pertaining to its report.

b.   If evidence is placed before the General Committee to its satisfaction that undue influence has been exercised by any person, or that any improper means have been adopted to obtain, or interfere with, the appointment of a Judge or the participation by any dog at any Trial under Kennel Club Regulations, the General Committee may require all correspondence and evidence in connection with the case to be produced in order that it may deal with the offenders under Rule A42 of the Rules of the Kennel Club.

15. Fines and Penalties

The General Committee shall have power to fine any person for breaches of Kennel Club Regulations subject to a right of appeal, notice of intention of which must be lodged within fourteen days from the date on which the decision is given, and subject to the prescribed appeal process as shall be determined by the General Committee from time to time. In the event of such fines not being paid within the time stipulated by the General Committee, that person may, at the discretion of the General Committee, be dealt with as if a complaint under Kennel Club Rule A42 had been lodged and proved to the satisfaction of the General Committee.

J(A)
THE MANAGEMENT, CONDUCT AND JUDGING OF FIELD TRIALS

a.   A Field Trial should be run as nearly as possible to an ordinary day's shooting.

b.   All Competitors, Judges and Officials must be present when the Secretary or Chief Steward has announced the Trial has commenced or when the Trial is deemed to have commenced.

c.   The Chief Steward should liaise closely with the Steward of the Beat who will have planned which ground is to be used for the Trial. He or she should, where necessary, welcome all on behalf of the society and introduce the Host, Steward of the Beat, Judges, Guns and other officials. The Chief Steward, moreover, should explain the outline of the day, with instructions about transport, lunch, toilets and other arrangements. The Chief Steward should also issue warnings on safety.

d.   At the end of the day, the Chief Steward should ensure that the Host, Guns, Judges and officials are properly thanked.

e.   Dogs must not wear any form of collar when under the orders of the Judges except for identification where necessary.

f.   Dogs must be excluded from further participation in the Stake if they have committed an 'eliminating fault'. The Judges may also discard dogs for 'major faults'. Where a dog is eliminated for 'hard mouth' all the Judges must have examined the injured game before the dog is discarded. The handler shall also be given the opportunity of examining the game in the presence of the Judges, but the decision of the Judges is final.

2. Water Tests

a.   A Water Test requires a dog to enter water readily and swim to the satisfaction of the Judges.

b.   If a separate Water Test is included as part of a Stake, all dogs placed in the awards must have passed this test.

c. A handler is not entitled to ask for a shot to be fired. Where a Special Water Test is conducted for part qualification for the title of Field Trial Champion (in accordance with the provisions of Kennel Club Regulations for entries in the Stud Book, Champions, and Warrants, paragraphs K2.c), it must be held between September 1 and April 1 inclusive.

3. Judging

a. The task of the Judges is to find the dog which, on the day, pleases them most by the quality of its work from the shooting point of view. They must, therefore, take natural game-finding to be of the first importance in Field Trials. A Judge must also have a very good working knowledge of the breed or breeds under Trial and have the interest and future of the breed or breeds at heart, since final placings may influence breeding plans and so determine the course of breed development.

b. No Judge should accept an invitation to judge a Trial, and no competitor should enter a Trial, unless they are fully conversant with the current Field Trial Regulations. The Chief Steward of a Field Trial should ensure that each of the Judges at a Field Trial has a copy of the current Field Trial Regulations.

c. Judges are responsible for the proper conduct of the Trial in accordance with Kennel Club Rules and Field Trial Regulations and the Schedule for the Stake. Judges are also expected to maintain and abide by the highest standards in accordance with the appropriate Codes of Best Practice as published from time to time.

d. All Judges, Chief Stewards and others responsible for the organization of the Trial should be courteous and co-operative with the Host and Steward of the Beat and fall in with their arrangements to achieve the best result possible in an atmosphere of friendliness and confidence.

e. At the start of the day, the Judges should be introduced to each other and decide their positions in the line which will remain the same throughout the body of the Stake. The Judges should brief the Guns and handlers and if, at any time, conditions force them to depart from the arrangements they have set out, the Chief Steward should be informed so that he or she can advise the competitors, Guns and others affected.

f. Judges should also make themselves aware of any special prizes which are to be awarded in the Stake.

g. Judges should ask the Steward of the Beat what the game position is likely to be and regulate the amount of work or number of retrieves for each dog accordingly. At driven Trials Judges should, after consultation with the Steward of the Beat, ensure that dogs sitting at a drive are positioned as to have the best opportunity to retrieve runners or wounded game during the drive. They should also satisfy themselves that arrangements have been made for the collection of dead or wounded game not gathered by the competing dogs and where necessary its humane despatch.

h. Judges should make sure that they have the correct dogs in the line.

i. Judges should be careful for the safety of dogs and should not require them to negotiate hazards such as dangerous barbed wire fences, ice on ponds, unsupervised roadways or walls with high drops. Whilst Judges should take reasonable precautions for the safety of competing dogs, it is also the duty of the handler to satisfy himself or herself that their dog is suitably trained, physically fit and prepared to undertake the work allocated by the Judges before directing it to carry out the task specified.

j. A higher standard of work is expected in Stakes which carry a qualification for the title of Field Trial Champion.

k. All Judges must certify on the Game Certificate that they have been satisfied that the conditions at the Stake were such as to enable the dogs to be satisfactorily tested. If there is not sufficient game the Stake must be considered void.

l. It is the duty of the Judges to give dogs every opportunity to work well by seeing that conditions are, as far as possible, in their favour. In all Trials the work of the dog is much affected by the way the handler behaves. Noisy handling, however occasioned, is a major fault. A good handler will appear to do little but watch his dog while maintaining at all times perfect control over it.

m. Judges should keep their opinions strictly to themselves and act on what happens on the day or days of the Trial at which they are judging, forgetting past performance.

n. At the end of each retrieve or run, Judges are advised to place each dog in a category such as A or B (+ or −) according to the work done. Such gradings may, quite properly, be supplemented on occasion by additional notation for reference purposes when Judges are going through their books. It is, however, imperative to appreciate that gradings must never be retrospectively adjusted. Neither should there ever be any attempt to sum sequences of grades to produce a single letter grading of a dog. When all dogs have been seen by a Judge, or Judges, they will wish to confer to determine which dogs they wish to discard or retain; it is vitally important for Judges to make short notes of each dog's work. Judges should never expect to be able to trust to memory.

o. Judges on the A Panel should bear in mind that they will be asked for assessments of B Panel or non-panel Judges with whom they officiate.

4. For all Sub-groups Required to Retrieve

a. A dog should be steady to shot and fall of game and should retrieve tenderly to hand on command. Handlers shall not send their dog until directed by the Judge.

b. Judges at Open Stakes and Championships should ask their Guns not to shoot directly over a dog when it is already out working on a retrieve.

   In other Stakes, Judges should ask their Guns not to shoot when a dog is already out working on a retrieve unless by so doing they are certain there would be no chance of distracting the dog from its task.

c. All wounded game should, where possible, be gathered and/or despatched immediately. Unless exceptional circumstances prevail then wounded game should always be tried for before dead game. If game cannot be gathered, the Judge must depute this task to the official handler and dog appointed for this purpose.

d. If game is shot very close to a dog which would make a retrieve of no value, the retrieve may be offered to a dog under another Judge.

e. Handlers should be instructed where to try from and be given reasonable directions as to where the game fell. If the dogs tried fail to complete the retrieve the Judges should search the area of fall and, if they find the game, the dogs tried, save in exceptional circumstances, will be eliminated. However, should a dog or dogs prove to have been tried in the wrong area they should not be so penalized.

f. Good marking is essential in a retrieving dog as it should not disturb ground unnecessarily. Judges should give full credit to a dog which goes straight to the fall and gets on with the job. Similarly, the ability to take the line of a hare, wounded rabbit or bird should be credited.

g. A good retrieve will include a quick and unfussy pick-up followed by a fast return. The handler should not have to snatch or drag game from the dog's mouth. Whilst Judges should not penalize a dog too heavily for putting game down to get a firmer grip, they must never, however, condone sloppy retrieving. A good game-finding dog should not rely on the handler to find the game. It should, however, be obedient and respond to its handler's signals where necessary.

   Dogs showing game-finding ability and initiative when hunting and retrieving should be placed above those which have to be handled to their game. Usually, the best dog seems to require the least handling. It appears to have an instinctive knowledge of direction and makes a difficult find look simple and easy.

h. If a dog is performing indifferently on a runner, it must be called up promptly. If more dogs are tried on the runner, the work of all these dogs must be assessed in relation to the order in which they are tried. The handlers of the second and subsequent dogs down may be allowed to take their dogs towards the fall, as may the handler of the first dog if it has not had a chance to mark the game. Game picked by the second or a subsequent dog constitutes an 'eye wipe'. Dogs which have had their eyes wiped during the body of the Stake, however it may have occurred, will be discarded. All eye wipes should be treated on their merits. If the first dog sent shows ability by acknowledging the fall and making a workmanlike job of the line or the area, it need not automatically be barred from the awards by failing to produce the game provided that the game is not collected by another dog tried by the Judges, or by the Judges themselves, when searching the area which they directed the handler to search. Moreover, there will be occasions when circumstances make it impossible to send a dog promptly. If this happens and a significant delay ensues, a dog disadvantaged in this way should not be penalized as a first dog down.

i. All game should be examined for signs of hard mouth. A hard-mouthed dog seldom gives visible evidence of hardness. The dog will simply crush in one or both sides of the ribs. Visible inspection and blowing up the feathers on a bird will not disclose the damage, digital examination is imperative. Place the game on the palm of the hand, breast upwards, head forward, and feel the ribs with fingers and thumb. They should be round and firm. If they are caved in or flat this may be evidence of hard mouth. Be sure the game reaches the co-Judges for examination. Judges should always satisfy themselves that the damage done has been caused by the dog, not by the shot or fall. Judges, for instance, must be clear about the difference between damage to the ribcage caused by shot and the quite distinctive damage caused by a dog. Handlers must be given the opportunity of inspecting the damaged game in the presence of the Judges, but the decision of the Judges is final. A sure sign of good mouth is a dog bringing in live game whose head is up and eye bright. Superficial damage, if any, in this case can be ignored. At times, the rump of a strong runner may be gashed and look ugly. Care should be taken here, as it may be the result of a difficult capture or lack of experience in mastering a strong runner by a young dog. There should be no hesitation or sentiment with hard mouth. The dog must be eliminated.

Annex B to J Regulations
J(B)
RETRIEVERS

1. Introduction

a. *Basic Requirements*

Dogs shall be required to be steady by the handler whilst being shot over until commanded to quest for dead or wounded game, from land or water, and retrieve tenderly to hand. Any dog which does not fulfil the basic requirements shall not receive an award or a Certificate of Merit.

b. *Number of Runners*

With the exception of the Retriever Championship, to qualify for entry in the Kennel Club Stud Book, the number of runners permitted in Stakes is as follows:

(1) Two-day Open Stakes: maximum 24, minimum 20.

(2) One-day Open Stakes: maximum 12, minimum 10.

(3) Other Stakes per day: maximum 16, minimum 10.

c. *Competing*

(1) The order of running shall be the order of the draw unless, in exceptional circumstances with the Judges approval it is decided to split the competitors.

(2) Initially, the dog with the lowest number under each Judge should be placed on the Judge's right. When there are three Judges for a Stake they must judge singly and when there are four Judges they must judge in pairs. If two of the four Judges are not Panel Judges they must not judge together. Moreover, if there are only two A Panel Judges present they must not judge together.

(3) All dogs, unless discarded, must be tried in the first two rounds by more than one Judge if there are three Judges, or by more than one pair of Judges if there are four. Whether the Trial is run in numerical order or split in exceptional circumstances dogs must not come into line in the second round under the same Judges as in the first round. After the second round, dogs may be called back into line in numerical order to either side in a four Judge system or to any Judge in a three Judge system.

(4) In the event that the dogs are to be split between the Judges, this will be done odds and evens. Where the Trial is to be run under the four judge system, in the first round the odd numbered dogs will be seen by the right-hand judges

and the evens by the left-hand judges. Where this system is adopted, in the second round the odd-numbered dogs remaining in the Trial must be seen by the left-hand judges and the evens by the right-hand judges. The Judges can thereafter continue to rotate the dogs remaining in the stake in this way until they get together for a run-off, when the order of sending shall revert to numerical order.

(5) Where the Trial is to be run under the three judge system, the dogs should be split equally, and in numerical order, between the three judges, i.e. 1, 2, 3, 4 with the right-hand judge, 5, 6, 7, 8 with the middle judge and 9, 10, 11 and 12 with the left-hand judge in a 12 dog stake and 1–8, 9–16 and 17–24 in a two day. Dogs should then rotate from right to left so that the dogs under the left-hand judge in the first round should be seen by the right-hand judge next and so on. The rotation should continue until a run-off when numerical order will resume.

d. *Credit Points*

Natural game finding ability.

Drive and style.

Good retrieving and delivery.

Quickness in gathering game.

Control.

Quiet handling.

Nose.

Marking ability.

e. *Eliminating Faults*

Hard mouth.

Running in.

Failing to enter water.

Changing game whilst retrieving.

Without merit.

Whining or barking.

Out of control.

Refusal to retrieve.

Chasing.

f. *Major Faults*

Unsteadiness at heel.

Disturbing ground.

Slack and unbusinesslike work.

Noisy or inappropriate handling.

Being eye wiped.

Poor control.

Failing to find dead or wounded game.

Sloppy retrieving and delivery.

2. Trial Procedure

a. *The Three Judge System*

If there is one A Panel Judge, then it is advisable that he or she takes the centre of the line, to be available to the other Judges if required, and be able to keep some contact with all the line.

b. *The Four Judge System*

If there are only two A Panel Judges they should not judge together.

c. *The Line*

(1) In walked-up trials the Steward of the Beat will be in charge of the line and dictate the pace of the line.

(2) In a three Judge walked-up Trial, the Judges will be positioned left, centre and right. Each Judge will usually have two Guns shooting for him and he would normally place himself and his dogs between his Guns. If there are extra Guns then it should be decided which Judge they are to shoot for. This will go a long way towards avoiding two dogs being sent for the same game.

d. (1) Dogs must walk steadily at heel and sit quietly at drives.

(2) If the game situation permits, two retrieves in the first round, then one retrieve in the second round is the usual procedure. It is imperative that the Chief Steward should be informed of any dogs eliminated or discarded for any reason. This will enable the Chief Steward to have the correct dogs available when required. It is, however, the Judge or Judge's responsibility to ensure that the right dogs are in line.

(3) The Chief Steward should send in the second round dogs to the appropriate Judge when there is a vacancy in the line (paragraph J(B)1.c refers). Second round dogs should have their opportunity to be tried against first round dogs when the situation arises.

(4) A Judge should be most careful to see that each dog gets its chance in the correct order, starting with the lowest number on the right. Should dog No. 1 fail, and dog No. 2 be successful, so eliminating his partner, No. 2 still has the first chance on the next retrieve. In these circumstances a dog may be given two consecutive retrieves.

(5) When a Judge tries his dogs, for example No. 1 and No. 2, behind other dogs, if No. 1 dog is successful, then the next retrieve under that Judge should be offered to No. 2 dog. If the two dogs fail on game, the Judge should not call fresh dogs into the line to try for the retrieve until all the other dogs already in the line have been tried. In the concluding stages of a Trial, Judges may use their own discretion as the situation arises.

(6) In walked-up Trials if one part of the line is starved of game and the dogs have been down under that Judge or Judges for quite some time then another Judge or Judges, who may have been getting more game shot by their guns, could offer one or more of his Guns to the Judge or Judges who are short of game. The handlers should be made aware of these arrangements. It is quite unfair in the body of the Trial for a Judge to offer dead game to a co-Judge whilst asking their own dogs to try for the runners.

(7) A first dog failure is when the first dog to be tried on a retrieve, fails. However, if there is any significant delay in sending a dog, then it should not be penalized as a first dog failure when the game is not subsequently picked by another dog, tried by the Judges, or by the Judges searching the area which the handler has been directed to search.

e. *Run-off*

When the Judges decide to run off the top few dogs to confirm their final placings, they will usually position themselves together in the centre of the line or, at least, in a position where they can see all the dogs working. At this stage in the Trial, a dog may be stretched to such a degree that it may fail and be eye-wiped. In this situation the dog which has had its eye wiped would be penalized, but could still feature in the awards.

f. *Multiple handling*

If two or more dogs are handled by the same person:

(1) In a walked up Trial the accepted practice is for the handler to have his lowest numbered dog in line with his other dog or dogs on the lead held by a deputy out of the line, but in reasonably close proximity at the discretion of the Judges. On leaving the line the handler should exchange the dog with the deputy for his next lowest numbered dog and return to the line when instructed to do so by the Judges or dog steward.

(2) In a driven Trial a handler who has more than one dog may be expected to have all his dogs in line at a drive. A deputy should be in reasonably close proximity at the discretion of the Judges and the handler, ready to put the other dog or dogs on the lead should the handler be asked to send one of the dogs for a retrieve during the drive. At the end of the drive all dogs, other than the dog which the Judges wish to try next in its turn, should be taken out of line and should be held by the deputy on the lead until required in line. When directed to do so by the Judges, the handler should exchange the dog in line with the deputy for his next lowest numbered dog and re-run to the line when instructed to do so by the Judges or dog steward.

(3) These procedures apply not only in the body of the Stake, but also in the run off.

Annex C to J Regulations
J(C)
SPANIELS

1. Basic Requirements

Dogs shall be required to quarter ground hunting for game and other quarry species (hereafter game), to be steady to flush, shot and fall and to retrieve tenderly to hand on command. Any dog which does not fulfil these basic requirements shall not receive an award or a Certificate of Merit.

2. Number of Runners

The number of runners permitted in Stakes to qualify for entry in the Kennel Club Stud Book is as follows:

    a.   Open Stakes – maximum 18, minimum 14.

    b.   Other Stakes – maximum 18, minimum 12.

    c.   Spaniel (Cocker) and Spaniel (English Springer) Championships – no maximum number. Open Spaniel Stakes are presently confined to Spaniels (Cocker) and Spaniels (English Springer).

3. Competing

Where possible dogs should be run in pairs, one dog under each Judge or pair of Judges. In the first round, odd numbers will run under the right-hand Judge(s) in consecutive order and, unless eliminated or discarded, will run in the second round under the left-hand Judge(s) and vice versa. A handler who is running two dogs in the Stake may already be running a dog when called for a run with his or her other dog. The Judge(s) should then call the next dog on that side to allow continuity of the Stake. When this occurs the Stake must revert to the original running order at the earliest opportunity. After the second round of a Stake is completed the Judges may call up any dogs they please and in any order.

4. Credit Points

Natural game-finding ability.	Marking ability.
Drive.	Style.
Control.	Quiet handling.
Clean quick retrieving and good delivery.	

5. Eliminating Faults

Hard mouth.	Whining or barking.
Missing game on the beat.	Running in or chasing.
Failing to enter water.	Refusal to retrieve.
Out of control.	Picking wrong retrieve.
Being eye wiped.	Changing game whilst retrieving.
Without merit.	

6. Major Faults

Disturbing ground.	Poor control.
Catching healthy game.	Not stopping to flush.
Noisy handling.	Not quartering or making ground good.
Not stopping to shot and game.	
Failing to find dead or wounded game (subject to J(A)4.h.).	

7. Trial Procedure

A Spaniel's first job is to hunt and find game and flush it within range of the handler. A Spaniel should at all times work within range with good treatment of ground and must not miss game on the beat it is working. During this period, the Judge(s) can assess the game-finding ability, pace, drive, and, possibly, courage. A dog should have drive and face cover well, but at the same time, should be lively and biddable. In short it should be exciting and a pleasure to watch. It should show good treatment of ground with a minimum of help from its handler. All things being equal, the stylish dog should be given credit. However, Judge(s) should be satisfied that the fast stylish dog is also the best game finder. The direction of the wind has a considerable influence on the way a dog will work ground. With a head-on wind the dog should quarter the ground systematically, left to right and vice versa, making good all likely game-holding cover, but keeping within gunshot distance of the handler. With a following wind it could be very different. The dog will often want to pull well out, then work back towards the handler. Judge(s) must regulate the pace of the line to allow the dog to do this and make good its ground. When hunting, lines and foot scents should be ignored. Persistent pulling on foot scents is unprofitable and can result in game being missed. However, the ability to take the line to a shot rabbit or hare and birds which have run should be credited. A run without a find should not automatically bar a dog from the final placings.

8. Any game caught by a dog whilst hunting must be retrieved to its handler and handed to the Judge(s) for despatch. After examination the Judge(s) may discard the dog unless there are extenuating circumstances.

9. It is a refinement if a dog indicates the presence of game before flushing the game positively.

10. A dog should stop to flush, game and shot, but if it moves in order to mark the fall, if this is obscured, this shows intelligence and should be credited.

11. A Spaniel should pick up cleanly, return quickly and deliver tenderly to hand. Such a retrieve is desirable; but too much should not be made of a momentary check if the dog has had a long gruelling hunt up to the time of flushing, thus making the retrieve possible. This should be allowed for. Whenever possible, and always bearing the conditions in mind, a dog should not be sent on a long unseen retrieve, but should be taken to within a reasonable distance of the fall. Normally, it is unwise to try more than two dogs on one retrieve. If both dogs are tried and fail to complete the retrieve and the Judges have satisfactorily searched the area, the line will continue to move forward. Should any subsequent dog find dead or wounded game, however, this will not necessarily be considered to be an eye-wipe.

12. Judges should refrain from holding a conversation with anyone whilst a dog is actively competing. From the moment the dog starts working, Judges should make every effort to keep the dog in view. When the dog is sent out for a retrieve, the Judges should also, where possible, observe the dog's every move until the game is delivered to hand.

13. Judges are under an obligation never to waste game and if a spare retrieve becomes available it must be offered in the first instance to the dog on the other side, if this dog has not yet had a retrieve. The Judges may subsequently offer a spare retrieve to a dog that has already had a satisfactory run without a retrieve in sequence starting with the lowest number.

14. Run-Off
It is desirable to place the dogs on their work in the body of the Stake. If the Judges are unable to do this then the dogs may be further assessed by running them side by side. The main consideration now should be style, pace, ground treatment and each dog's response to its handler. Judges must ensure that competitors do not interfere with the other handler or dog (Regulation J9.b(5)). In this run-off stage dogs will only be discarded if they commit eliminating faults.

Annex D to J Regulations
J(D)
Pointers and Setters

1. **Basic Requirements**
Dogs shall be required to quarter ground systematically with pace and style in search of gamebirds, to point gamebirds, to be steady to flush and shot and, where applicable, to fall. Dogs should not be gun shy. The dog should work its point out freely, on command, without the handler either touching the dog or moving in front of it. Any dog which does not fulfil the basic requirements shall not receive an award or a Certificate of Merit.

2. Number of Runners

To qualify for entry in the Kennel Club Stud Book, the number of runners permitted in stakes is as follows:

a. Champion Stake and Open Stakes: maximum 40, minimum 12.

b. Novice/All Aged Stakes: maximum 45, minimum 12.

c. Puppy Stakes: maximum 45, minimum 8.

Where an Open and any other type of stake are to run on the same day, the maximum number of runners over the whole day is 45.

3. Competing

Dogs are to be run in pairs and their handlers must walk within a reasonable distance of one another as though shooting together. Dogs should be placed as drawn on the card, with the first number on the left, and every dog must be brought up in its proper turn without delay.

4. Draws

Prior to the Stake and before the commencement of each round a draw will be made. For second and subsequent rounds, if the Judges are satisfied that they have identified the dogs which will figure in the awards, they may run them in pairs as they see fit, to establish the final places. When a handler has more than one dog in a Stake, those dogs shall, when a draw takes place, be kept separate in every round.

5. Byes

When in any round in a Stake the number of dogs is unequal, the dog whose number is drawn last must be run against a dog chosen by the Judges. No dog shall have a second such bye.

6. Collars

The Judges may require any dogs to wear distinguishing collars.

7. The whole quality of a dog's work must be taken into consideration, not just the number of points it has made. The Judges should be looking for credit qualities rather than trying to eliminate dogs, and it is the better dogs which should be fully tried, not wasting ground and time on those with little or no merit. Minor faults should not be too heavily penalized when a dog has done good sound work. A dog's work should be exciting and a pleasure to watch, as would appeal to and interest guns particularly if gamebirds are scarce.

8. Credit Points

Systematically quartering with stamina pace and style.

Style on point and production.

Dropping to wing.

Hunting with drive and purpose.

Natural backing.

Quiet handling.

9. Eliminating Faults

Flushing up wind.

Chasing fur or feather.

Whining or barking.

Stealing a point.

Not dropping to flush down wind.

Without merit.

Out of control.

Unsteadiness to game.

Blinking a point.

Interfering with the other dog on point.

Missing gamebirds on the beat.

10. Major Faults

Poor ground treatment.

Stickiness on point.

Persistent back casting.

Noisy handling.

Persistent false pointing.

11. Each brace should be tried for a reasonable time except when undoubted lack of merit of one or both dogs is confirmed by both Judges.

12. The dog should quarter the appointed ground as drawn with pace and style making good all its ground, working correctly to the wind particularly if downwind or cheek wind, showing gamebird finding ability and working naturally with the minimum of handling. Dogs should be steady to fur, feather, flush and shot.

13. If a dog flushes a gamebird upwind it should be discarded, but if it is working downwind and flushes, or on the first cast runs sideways into gamebirds and drops immediately, having had no chance to wind them, these do not constitute eliminating faults.

14. Judges should appreciate that a backing dog may be disadvantaged in the following circumstances:

If a pointing dog is sticky on point.

If a pointing dog is guilty of persistent false pointing.

If a pointing dog is not positive in its workout.

15. When a dog has worked ground and gamebirds are proved to have been left on the beat, that dog has missed gamebirds and should be eliminated. If gamebirds are found on the ground which the dog should have worked but did not cover, the Judges should consider the circumstances before penalizing the dog for faulty ground treatment (but not for missing gamebirds).

16. If, when pointing gamebirds, a dog blinks by leaving the point and continues hunting, that dog must be discarded.

17. Judges should appreciate that different breeds have different styles of working and should make themselves conversant with these styles.

18. Judges should conserve the ground by being as decisive as possible. They should keep up with the handlers to try to see everything that takes place, but not try to keep up with a dog that is obviously running out of its ground.

19. If possible, it is desirable that the winner should have run with the second, and the third with the fourth, to minimize the luck of the draw regarding variations in conditions, scent and gamebird supply.

Annex E to J Regulations
J(E)
Breeds which Hunt, Point and Retrieve

1. Basic Requirements
Dogs shall be required to quarter ground systematically in search of quarry (hereafter game), to point game, to flush on command, to be steady to flush, shot and fall, and to retrieve tenderly to hand on command from land and water. Any dog which does not fulfil the basic requirements shall not receive an award or a Certificate of Merit.

2. Number of Runners
With the exception of the Hunt, Point and Retrieve Championship, to qualify for entry in the Kennel Club Stud Book, the number of runners permitted in
Stakes is as follows:
a.   Open Stakes: maximum 12, minimum 10.
b.   Other Stakes: maximum 12, minimum 8.

3. The Trial should run as nearly as possible to an ordinary day's rough shooting for a small party of guns, numbering not more than four in total.

4. Competing
Dogs shall be run singly in order of the draw under two Judges judging as a pair. A dog, unless discarded must have been tried at least twice in the line, and complete a water test on the day of the trial, before it may receive an award or certificate of merit.

5. Credit Points
Systematically quartering with stamina, pace and style. Hunting with drive and purpose.
Style on point and production.   Good marking.
Dropping to wing.   Quiet handling.
Speed and efficiency in retrieving.   Good water work.

6. Eliminating Faults
Hard mouth.   Whining or barking.
Flushing up wind.   Out of control.
Unsteadiness.   Running in or chasing.
Failure to hunt or point.   Blinking a point.
Changing game whilst retrieving.   Being eye-wiped.
Picking the wrong retrieve.   Refusal to retrieve or swim.
Missing game on the beat (excluding hare and snipe). Without merit.

7. Major Faults
Poor ground treatment.   Stickiness on point.
Persistent false pointing.   Disturbing ground
Not stopping to flush down wind.   Noisy handling.

Not acknowledging game going away.   Catching unwounded game.

Failing to find dead or wounded game (subject to J(A)4.h.).

8. Judges should define the beat to be worked. As much discretion as is practical should be left to the handler as to how to work the ground.

9. Judges must judge as a pair, but record their assessments independently having established the categories to be marked. They should see as much work as possible from every dog, particularly those which impress most favourably, and assess this work carefully in every aspect. Judges should remember that the main work of a dog which hunts, points and retrieves is to find game, and present it to the Guns so that they have a good chance of a reasonable shot. Particular note should be taken of the following:

a. *Game Finding Ability.* This is of the highest importance. The Judge must assess game-finding by observing the way the dog works its beat with regard to the wind, covers all likely game-holding pockets, and responds to scent generally, and also by its drive and sense of purpose.

b. *Ground Treatment.* In all stakes it is highly desirable that all dogs be worked into the wind wherever possible. Dogs should quarter the beat systematically and with purpose, regulating their pace to suit the type of ground and cover. If a dog flushes game upwind it should be discarded, but if it is working downwind and flushes or runs sideways into game having had no chance to wind it, these do not constitute eliminating faults. However, the dog should always acknowledge game so flushed and stop.

c. *Pointing.* Credit will be given to the dog that acknowledges game scent positively, draws in deliberately, points staunchly, flushes only on command and is subsequently steady. Persistent, false or unproductive pointing is a major fault. False pointing may be recognized by the dog leaving its point and immediately showing no further interest in the scent that apparently brought it on point. Unproductive pointing is where the dog points residual scent. Less experienced dogs tend to persist on such unproductive points, thereby wasting time, whereas a more experienced dog will recognize this residual scent for what it is and quickly resume hunting. If, when pointing game, a dog blinks by leaving the point and continues hunting, that dog must be eliminated.

d. *Retrieving.* All retrieves should be completed as quickly as possible so that the progress of the Trial is not interrupted unduly.

e. *Style.* Before final assessments of the work are made, Judges should consider the style of the dogs. Credit should be given to a dog which embraces grace of movement, stylishness when pointing and retrieving and which shows keenness and competence in what it is doing. Judges should recognize that each breed within the Hunt, Point and Retrieve sub-group has its own individual style, and they should acquaint themselves with these differences.

10. Water Retrieves

a. In Open and All-Aged Stakes, the water retrieve is a blind retrieve from across water. If a dog returns by land, it should not be penalized for this unless it wastes time thereby.

b. In Novice Stakes, the water retrieve is a marked retrieve from water with a shot fired.

c. To receive an award, normally a dog must complete a Water Test on the day of the Trial. If, due to unforeseen circumstances, a Water Test cannot take place, or when there are no facilities for a Water Test nearby, a potential award winner may take a Special Water Test allied to that Trial, at a later date, conducted by two Judges, one of whom must be on the A panel. Having been given a blank Special Water Certificate, it will be the responsibility of the handler of a potential award winner to get the dog tested within three weeks of the Trial. The Water Test may take place at another Trial or independently by arrangement with two Judges. Upon successful completion of a Special Water Test, the handler should send the signed

Certificate back to the organizing society's Field Trial Secretary who should then forward it on to the Kennel Club so that the award can be confirmed. The organizing society must notify the Kennel Club that this special arrangement is taking place.

Annex F to J Regulations
J(F)
SHOW GUNDOG WORKING CERTIFICATE

1. The Show Gundog Working Certificate is not a qualification in itself, however, when awarded it enables the 'Sh' to be removed from the title of Show Champion. In no circumstances can the letters SGWC be placed after a dog's name.

2. A gundog which has won a Challenge Certificate or previously qualified for Crufts through a breed class may be entered for a Show Gundog Working Certificate at a Field Trial or a Show Gundog Working Day for its sub-group, licensed by the Kennel Club, with a minimum of two Judges officiating, of which at least one must be an A Panel Judge.

3. The permission of the society holding the Trial must be obtained and the dog must be entered on the entry form of the meeting. The fee charged by the society should be the same as that for dogs entering the Trial.

4. Societies which are registered with the Kennel Club and which have been authorized to organize Field Trials may apply for permission to organize a Show Gundog Working Day for their relevant sub-group.

5. Retrieving breeds should be tested on freshly shot, unhandled game.

6. The granting of a Show Gundog Working Certificate shall be at the discretion of the Judges at the meeting and all Judges must sign the Certificate.

7. Before signing a Certificate the Judges must be satisfied that the dog fulfilled the following requirements:
    a. The dog has been tested in line.
    b. The dog has shown that it is not gun shy.
    c. For a Retriever, that it hunted for, and found, dead or wounded game, faced cover, and retrieved tenderly.
    d. For a Spaniel, that it hunted, faced cover, produced game and retrieved tenderly.
    e. For a Pointer or Setter that it hunted and pointed game.
    f. For a Hunt, Point and Retrieve Breed that it hunted, pointed game and retrieved tenderly.
    g. For all retrieving breeds, that the dog entered water freely, swam and retrieved. If a natural retrieve from water is not possible, then a dummy may be used and if suitable water is not available the dog is permitted to undertake a Special Water Test as soon as possible after the day, but between 1 September and 1 April, which will be recognized by the issue of a Certificate, to be signed by two Field Trial Panel Judges, one of whom must be on the 'A' Panel.
    h. That the dog has not whined or barked in line, subject to the Breed Standard.
    i. That the dog has been under reasonable control; absolute steadiness is not essential.

8. Judges should be aware of their responsibility when awarding a SGWC, that the dog has been thoroughly tested, and shown sufficient merit to become a Champion. (Regulation J(A)3.a. refers.)

Annex G to J Regulations
J(G)
KENNEL CLUB REGULATIONS FOR GUNDOG WORKING TESTS

These Regulations should be read alongside and assume a familiarity with, Kennel Club Field Trial Regulations. A copy of these Regulations must be available at all Gundog Working Tests (GWTs.)

1. Introduction

a. GWTs are competitions which, by artificially simulating shooting day conditions, seek to assess, without game being shot, the working abilities of the various breeds of Gundog. Cold Game and dummies may be used at the discretion of the organizers.

b. No title used to describe the winners of GWTs will be associated with such competition which is best understood as a means to an end rather than an end in itself.

c. The Kennel Club authorizes Registered societies to hold competitive Gundog Working Tests.

d. Scurries, Pick-Ups, and other similar events are exempt, as are non-competitive Club Training Assessments where no places are on offer. The Kennel Club also recognizes that events involving unregistered dogs do sometimes take place. Such events cannot, however, be considered to be GWTs under these Regulations.

e. Application for authority to hold GWTs must be made annually to the Kennel Club and, on the form provided, applicants should give an indication of the number of GWTs held in the preceding year.

f. Unaffiliated societies or individuals may also be accorded annual authority to organize GWTs, subject to 1.e. above, and these must be run in accordance with the J(G) Regulations.

g. The GWT year will run from 2nd February to 1st February.

h. (1) Notwithstanding the provisions of these Regulations, certain events which are not authorized by the Kennel Club may from time to time be recognized by the General Committee of the Kennel Club. The General Committee is able to grant permission for Kennel Club registered dogs to be entered for such events.

(2) A Judge, competitor or promoter will not be prejudiced by participation in such unauthorized events.

2. Definition of Gundog Working Tests (GWT)

a. GWTs may be run for any of the three sub-groups of Gundogs recognized by the Kennel Club as detailed below:

(1) Retrievers and Irish Water Spaniels.

(2) Sporting Spaniels other than Irish Water Spaniels.

(3) Breeds which Hunt, Point and Retrieve.

b. The following classes of competition are recognized by the Kennel Club:

(1) OPEN. Open to all dogs of a specified breed or breeds, although preference may be given to dogs which have gained a place or certificate of merit at a Field Trial, been placed First, Second or Third in an Open GWT, or won a Novice GWT.

(2) NOVICE. Confined to dogs which have not gained a place or certificate of merit at a Field Trial, been placed First, Second or Third in an Open GWT or First in a Novice GWT held in accordance with Kennel Club Rules and Field Trial Regulations.

(3) PUPPY. Confined to dogs of specific breed or breeds less than eighteen months of age on the date of the test.

(4) UNCLASSIFIED. Open to all dogs of a specified breed or breeds, but may be restricted by conditions as determined by the society. To include Water and Team Tests. A Water Test can include dogs of any sub-group competing together. However, if dogs of more than one sub-group are competing as a Team, each sub-group will compete and be judged in accordance with the Kennel Club Gundog Working Test Regulations relating to that group.

3. Organization of Gundog Working Tests

a. The organization shall agree to hold and conduct the tests within the Rules and Regulations of the Kennel Club.

b. Control of Dogs. The owner, competitor, handler or other person in charge of a dog at Kennel Club authorized events must, at all times, ensure that the dog is kept under proper control whilst at the venue including its environs, car and caravan parks and approaches.

c. GWTs should be organized by a person or persons with experience of dog work under shooting field conditions. Each dog or team of dogs should have, as near as possible, an equal opportunity with any variability in circumstances, as far as possible, minimized.

d. The organizers of GWTs will try, wherever possible, to simulate the circumstances of a shooting day. They must also ensure the tests are designed to further good Gundog work, and not inhibit dogs from marking or showing natural working ability. It is important, for instance, that Guns and dummy throwers are positioned with such considerations in mind.

e.   The organizers must ensure that competitors are aware of the initial running order, and whether the GWT is to be conducted on cold game or dummies.

f.   Final decisions regarding the acceptability of tests lie with the Judge or Judges.

g.   Only dummies and dead game acceptable to the Judges, will be used for retrieves in GWTs.

h.   When dummies are thrown in association with gunfire in retrieving tests, the shot must always precede the thrown dummy and the gun should be positioned a plausible distance from the retrieve. With unseen retrieves gunfire is optional.

i.   A dog, when retrieving, must not be required to pass too close to another retrieve.

j.   Organizers and Judges must be careful for the safety of dogs and must not require them to negotiate dangerous obstacles. Whilst Judges should take reasonable precautions for the safety of competing dogs, it is the duty of the handler to satisfy himself or herself that the dog is suitably trained, physically fit and prepared to undertake the work allocated by the Judges before directing his or her dog to undertake the allotted task.

4. Conduct of Gundog Working Tests

a.   The organizers must ensure all competitors and Judges are informed that the event is being held under Kennel Club Rules and Field Trial Regulations.

b.   The Code of Conduct expected at GWTs is the same as that for Field Trials.

c.   Those taking part in GWTs shall not openly impugn the decision of the Judges or criticize the host, ground, or helpers. Any cases of alleged misconduct must be reported to the Kennel Club in accordance with Regulation J14 (Fraudulent and Discreditable Conduct at Trials). In particular the provisions of Field Trial Regulations J12 (Objections), J13 (Disqualification and Forfeit of Awards) and J15 (Fines and Penalties) shall apply.

d.   All dogs must be registered with the Kennel Club. Each dog to be of a breed included within the relevant sub-group as previously defined.

e.   The organizers have the power to exclude dogs from the competition and will have the right to refuse an entry.

f.   The organizers may restrict the numbers in a GWT, in which case the right to compete shall be decided by ballot.

g.   All Judges must have experience of dog-work under shooting field conditions.

h.   In an Open GWT, each sub-group must have at least one Kennel Club Field Trial Panel Judge officiating. All handlers must carry out the instructions of the Judges. The Judges are empowered to remove from the Test any dog whose handler does not follow their instructions or whose handler wilfully interferes with another competitor or his dog.

j.   No person attending a GWT may allow a bitch in season to be on the Test ground or foul any ground to be used by competing dogs.

k.   If, after consultation with the Judges, members of the committee present consider a dog unfit to compete by reason of contagious disease or physical condition, such a dog shall be required to be removed immediately from the ground. Any such case is liable to be reported to the Kennel Club.

l.   No dog shall wear a collar whilst competing.

m.   No person shall carry out punitive correction or harsh handling at a GWT.

n.   No competitor may withdraw their dog and leave the GWT ground without informing the Chief Steward.

5. Judging

a.   Judges must agree a common scoring system. All competitors should be informed of the scoring system at the commencement of a GWT. But, whatever the system adopted, failure to complete an individual test will result in a mark of zero. A multiple retrieve constitutes one test. If a dog fails or commits a serious fault in any part of a multiple exercise, this will result in a mark of zero for that exercise.

b. GWTs will typically be judged on a points system with individual tests marked out of 20, though on occasion, when their organization is more akin to that of a Field Trial, letter gradings may be used.

c. Judges must ensure that spectators are a reasonable distance from competitors in line.

d. Judges should give dogs every opportunity to work well by seeing that conditions are, as far as possible, in their favour. They will be looking for dogs which need the least handling and please them most from a shooting point of view.

e. In all retrieving breeds good marking is essential with a quick pick-up and a fast return. Judges will not penalize a dog too heavily for putting down a retrieve to get a firmer grip, but this must not be confused with sloppy retrieving.

f. Any serious fault or failure in an individual test or tests will disqualify a dog from gaining an individual award and may lead to elimination. In Team Tests, however, one dog's serious fault or failure will not disqualify a team from the awards. If two or more teams finish on equal points a run-off will be necessary to determine the result.

g. The Judges are empowered to withhold any prize or award if in their opinion competing dogs have not shown sufficient merit.

6. Instructions for Specific Sub-group Tests

a. **Retrievers**

(1) At the start of a GWT, Judges must ensure they have the correct dogs in the line, lowest number placed on the right.

(2) A Retriever must be steady to shot and fall and must retrieve only on command. Also, whenever possible, all dogs should be tested at a simulated drive, walking up and in water. A dog must walk steadily at heel.

(3) Good marking is essential with a quick pick-up and a fast return. Dogs should be credited for showing marking ability and initiative.

(4) If a dog fails a retrieve in the run-offs, it may still feature in the awards.

(5) *Credit Points*

Natural marking and hunting ability.	Quickness in gathering retrieve and delivery.
Nose.	Drive and style.
Quiet handling.	Control.

(6) *Serious Faults*

Refusing to retrieve.	Whining or barking.
Running in or chasing.	Out of control.
Changing retrieve.	Failing to enter water.
Poor heel work.	

b. **Spaniels**

(1) At the start of a GWT, Judges must ensure they have the correct dogs in the line. Dogs must be run either singly or in pairs, with the lowest number on the right.

(2) A Spaniel's primary task is to find game and flush within range of the handler. In GWTs it should at all times work within that range and demonstrate thorough ground treatment. The direction of the wind has a considerable influence on the way a dog works its ground. With a headwind the dog should quarter the ground systematically, making good all likely game-holding cover yet keeping within gunshot distance. With a following wind, the dog will often want to pull well out and then work back towards the handler. Judges must regulate the pace of the line to allow the dog to do this so that it can make good its ground. The Judge will assess the handling ability of the dog and also its pace, style, drive, courage and the quality of its ground treatment.

(3) A Spaniel must be steady to flush, shot and fall and retrieve on command from land or water.

(4) When dummies are thrown and gunfire used, the gun and dummy thrower must walk at the edge of the beat the dog is working in line with the handler.

(5) If a dog fails to retrieve in the run-offs, it may still feature in the awards.

(6) If live pigeons are released this must be treated as a separate exercise and not occur as part of an exercise involving a retrieve.

(7) *Credit Points*

Natural hunting ability.	Nose.
Good marking.	Drive.
Style.	Control.
Speed in gathering retrieve.	Delivery.
Quiet handling.	

(8) *Serious Faults*

Refusing to retrieve.	Whining or barking.
Running in or chasing.	Out of control.
Failing to enter water.	Changing retrieve.

c. Breeds which Hunt, Point and Retrieve

(1) Organizers must be aware of the limitations and possible problems when using game for pointing exercises.

(2) Dogs should quarter the beat across the wind hunting systematically and regulating their pace to suit the ground and cover. In Novice Tests dogs should not normally be required to work downwind.

(3) Judges must assess quartering, by observing the way the dog works its beat in relation to the wind. They should consider how the dog covers any possible game-holding pockets and its drive and style, especially as indicated by its response to the presence of scent.

(4) Retrieving tests must be set as naturally as possible and close distractions must be avoided.

(5) If a dog fails a retrieve in the run-offs, it may still feature in the awards.

(6) Dogs must be steady to shot and fall and retrieve on command.

(7) If live pigeons are released this must be treated as a separate exercise and not occur as part of an exercise involving a retrieve.

(8) *Credit Points*

Natural quartering and pointing ability.

Drive.	Style.
Good marking.	Control.
Quickness in gathering retrieve and delivery.	Quiet handling.

(9) *Serious Faults*

Refusing to retrieve. Whining or barking.

Out of control.	Chasing.
Failing to enter water.	Changing retrieve.

Appendix B

How to Complete a Field Trial Entry Form

The standard Field Trial entry form is in the main self-explanatory; however, some of the boxes are often incorrectly completed, and the following notes are intended to clarify what is required.

Note 1. In the case that two dogs are to be entered, the dog entered in this box will be taken as the 'preferred' dog and will be entered into a first ballot should this be necessary. If this is *not* to be the preferred dog then this should be explicitly stated by annotating the entry ***PREFERENCE ***

Note 2. It is of great help to the field trial secretary if the Stud Book number, if the dog has been issued with one, is entered here.

Note 3. If a second dog is to be entered, its details should be entered here. *See also* Note 1.

Note 4. Qualifications should be entered here when necessary to gain preference in a draw for All-Aged and Open stakes where prior performance will be taken into consideration. This box applies to Dog One only. Enter the highest award the dog has received.

Note 5. This box is to be completed with the highest award received by Dog Two, and should only be completed if a second dog is being entered into the trial. Do not use it to list any other awards Dog One may have received.

Gundog Society Name

ID No. 9999

Field Trial Entry Form

	Date		Entries Close:

Field Trial at: ....

Stake: ....

Entry Fees:

Members £20.00
Non Members £30.00

INSTRUCTIONS

Writing **MUST BE IN INK AND BLOCK CAPITALS**

This form must be used by one person only (or partnership).
Use one line only for each dog. The name of the dog and all the details as recorded with The Kennel Club must be given on this entry form. If an error is made the dog may be disqualified by the Committee of The Kennel Club. ENTRIES FOR FIELD TRIALS WILL ONLY BE ACCEPTED FROM GUNDOGS REGISTERED AT THE KENNEL CLUB IN THE GUNDOG GROUP (vide Regu J1a, 6a(l) & B20).
When entering more than one breed or variety, use if possible a separate form for each. On no account will entries be accepted without fees.

	REGISTERED NAME OF DOG (BLOCK CAPITALS)	KENNEL CLUB REGISTRATION NO, STUD BOOK NO OR ATC NO	FULL DATE OF BIRTH	BREEDER	SIRE (BLOCK LETTERS)	DAM (BLOCK LETTERS)
1		BREED	SEX			
2		BREED	SEX			

Qualification (see schedule)

	DATE	AWARD	STAKE	PROMOTING SOCIETY
1				
2				

ONE LINE FOR EACH DOG

CHECK ALL DETAILS BEFORE POSTING

DECLARATION

I/we agreed to submit to and be bound by The Kennel Club Rules and Regulations in their present form or as they may be amended from time to time in relation to all canine matters with which The Kennel Club is concerned.
I/we also undertake to abide by the Regulations of this Trial and not to bring to the Trial any dog which has contracted or been knowingly exposed to any infectious disease during the 21 days prior to the day of the Trial. I also declare that I am fully conversant with the Field Trial Regulations and have studied the guide to the conduct of field trials
I further declare that I believe to the best of my knowledge that the dogs are not liable to disqualification under Kennel Club Field Trials Rules and Regulations.

Usual Signature of Owner(s) .... Date ....
Note: Dogs entered in breach of Kennel Club Rules and Regulations are liable to disqualification whether or not the owner was aware of the breach.

Name of Owner(s) ....

Address ....

Tel/Fax No. ....

Entries and Fees which MUST BE PREPAID to be sent to:

Name of Handler (in block letters) ....

Address .... **Email** ....

Tel. No. .... **Fax No.** ....

Sample field trial entry form.

Index

Related Titles from Crowood

Barnes, Mike *The Game Shooting Handbook*

Bezzant, David *Hunting with Ferrets*

Bezzant, David *Rabbiting Terriers – their work and training*

Darling, John *Air Rifle Hunting*

Dear, N.C. *Hunt, Point, Retrieve Dogs for Work and Showing*

Frain, Seán *Rabbiting*

Hobson, J.C. Jeremy *Running a Shoot*

Hutcheon, Jon *Pigeon Shooting*

Potter, Lewis *Deer Stalking and Management*

Potts, Bruce *Sporting Rifles*

Reynolds, Mike *Shooting Made Easy*

Wright, Steve *Falconry*

Yardley, Michael *Positive Shooting*